ARIELLA NYSSA'S

self-love

bible

ARIELLA NYSSA'S
self-love
bible

Understand, love and celebrate
the most important person in your life:

you

murdoch books

Sydney | London

CONTENTS

HELLO ANGELS 6

Hello angels

Welcome to a safe place — a place where you can be honest and open with who you are and who you want to be. I'm Ariella, and I am passionate about bringing to light the importance of loving the person you are from the inside out.

Each of us is born unique. We are born innocently into a beautiful and wonderful world. But what happens? Where does our undying love for ourselves go?

As we grow up and find our feet in the world, experiences shape us. Our family, relationships and events trigger new elements of our personalities and can affect how we see ourselves. Maybe your parents' divorce or a toxic parental dynamic shaped your ideas and values about relationships. It may have been your inner child being stomped on and bullied throughout your schooling experience. It may have been childhood trauma, or losing someone really special to you. Maybe an eating disorder or mental health struggles played a huge part in your life and how you view yourself. Maybe you've just never really found yourself or begun to love yourself. No matter what brought you, this book is here to help you, to guide you in realising just how incredible you are and how much you have to offer the world.

From a young age we are taught by society that we are not enough. That we need to do all of these things, to look or act in a certain way and adhere to societal rules. To look better, do better, be better. It's time to get back to the core of who we are. To rejoice in the things that make each of us unique, that make us STAND OUT. To wholeheartedly LOVE ourselves on every level of our beings and enjoy this life.

What is self-love?

Society tells us that self-love is easy. It's as easy as having a skincare routine, drawing a bubble bath or reading a book. These things are incredible, don't get me wrong, but self-love is HARD. It's tiring, it's draining and sometimes it means delving into the hard times to learn and grow into a more accepting and loving human being. Self-love is being disciplined; it's being honest.

Self-love is digging deep down into ourselves and creating a life that we really want to be living.

It's chasing our hopes and dreams, working through the tough stuff and healing from whatever has torn us down.

I love using the chrysalis as a metaphor for self-love. A chrysalis is a transitional state for a caterpillar as it transforms into a butterfly. Butterflies go through a life cycle of four stages: egg, larva, pupa (chrysalis), imago (adult). To go through the final transformation, the caterpillar must stop eating and moving, hang upside down from a twig and mould itself into a shiny chrysalis made from its own body.

The chrysalis is iridescent in the sunlight and is a safeguard for the caterpillar, a protective casing that allows the insect to radically transform into its new self. The caterpillar doesn't need any outside help; it actually uses its own fluids to break itself down into cells called 'imaginal cells' (because they become the imago). These cells are then used to create a new identity.

Most people think that the 'end goal' of the chrysalis metaphor is that one day we will turn into a magical and beautiful butterfly. But when I first found out about the chrysalis, it stopped me dead in my tracks: self-love isn't a destination. It isn't an end goal. One day we won't wake up and magically be the butterflies we have always wanted to be. No.

As a baby and young child, I was comfortable in my own skin, but as I grew older I learned how to be a 'girly' girl and fit society's expectations.

Self-love is about the journey. It's about the growth and the changes we embark on. It's about using our own experiences, values and identity to find purpose and to be in this transitional state *always*. It's about constantly being a chrysalis. We will always be growing, healing and learning. And once we embrace this, we can unlock our inner beings and take on the world.

In my own self-love journey I've realised that a holistic approach is essential. It's not just about accepting your curves, lumps, bumps, marks, flub or belly rolls. It's about loving EVERYTHING: your personality, your spiritual beliefs, your goals and desires, your health, your sociability, your emotions, your relationships, your upbringing, your family, your past — EVERYTHING.

My story

I am about to tell you my story, a story that I didn't plan on and a story that nearly took my life. A story of my transition from a child full of love to a young adult lost and petrified of living, and finally to someone embracing who I am and not afraid to put myself out into a world that might reject me.

I want to state, before diving in, that I know I have lived a very privileged life. I am not marginalised or oppressed in my society for any reason, nor did I experience childhood trauma, as so many of you may have. If my story triggers you, I'm so sorry for the things you've experienced and I urge you to speak to a professional about them. I can only share from my own lived experience and I want to be completely honest about my journey.

As a child, I lived in a positive and warm environment. My family allowed me to be myself and I have very fond memories of this time. A huge aspect of my childhood was religion. I was taught to pray and was prayed for every night. In fact, I grew frightened if I forgot to pray at night. I was taken to church on Sundays and introduced to people from our religious community. My parents had strong religious values that they taught me, values centred around God and spirituality. It was all I ever knew. I was placed in a Christian school and my older sister, who was very religious, was my role model.

My parents were loving and accepting and, looking back, I think that if I had chosen a different route, they would have embraced me regardless. But because I had been taught that this was the 'right' way to live, it made it seem that anything else was 'wrong' or 'bad'. I didn't want to disappoint anyone in my family, so my people-pleasing tendencies began. As I grew up,

I focused less on myself and a lot on other people. I always wanted to make other people happy, which I've since realised isn't a bad thing in and of itself.

At school and in my community, I was surrounded by religious people, and although many were kind and caring, a lot of them were very judgemental. I became an ignorant young girl, only seeing the world from one perspective and judging anyone who thought differently. As I grew, I learned more about the backgrounds of my parents, family members and friends, and realised that while I'd thought everything was black and white, nothing is ever as simple as that.

I yearned to live more freely, but I was too fearful.

I still remember specific comments from close family friends, relatives and people in the Christian community that affected my confidence. When I was a child and was being my complete self, a lot of people put me down for it. For years, I minimised these comments. I thought it was silly that I remembered these things and dismissed them as nothing, especially compared with what others had been through. But they have shaped who I am today.

I was accepted into a performing arts high school, which opened up a whole new world for me. Suddenly I was meeting people who hadn't grown up in the church. And thus began another cycle of changing and morphing myself in an attempt to feel accepted. Puberty hit me early and fast, and my physical body started to come into play; my self-worth started to depend solely on my physical appearance. I became boy obsessed and began to go to house parties and even drink sometimes. I became egotistical, insecure and embarrassed about who I was. I often felt rejected, especially by boys.

After a few years of this, while at the summer church youth camp I went to every year, I found myself really getting along with a certain group of the young adults. They seemed to support me and want the best for me (or so I thought). While there, I had a huge breakthrough and 'gave my life' to Jesus.

When I was a child, my innocent and fearless behaviour was criticised by people around me. My confidence disappeared as religion made its mark on me.

This wasn't as radical as it sounds. I mean, I had grown up in the church. I had seen many people give their lives to Jesus over the years and I simply thought it was my time.

This was when my life began to really change. I made friends at church again, people who had known me from when I was little and felt so familiar. It seemed like they really cared about me. I was a young 16-year-old — vulnerable, afraid, insecure — and here was a group of people who were so welcoming, it seemed like a dream! I started getting involved in church — and I mean *really* involved. I would ditch my friends from school on the weekends to go to youth group, church services, conferences and Bible studies. Anything and everything related to the church.

In the beginning, these relationships were positive, loving and accepting but soon they grew toxic. The church had a lot of 'rules', and I say rules in quotation marks because they didn't call them rules. In fact, you had the freedom to do whatever you wanted as long as you had 'a relationship with God'. But really, this was not true. There was a lot of gossip, a lot of rumours and judgement coming from people about the decisions I was making in my life. I yearned to be a part of this clique, and to do so I thought I had to be the perfect Christian. I was trying to be like everyone else, but it meant being someone I was not. I stopped talking to boys, I stopped drinking and partying, I stopped hanging out with my school friends, I stopped wearing the clothes I wanted to wear or doing things that I wanted to do — things that were a part of me.

The pressure was immense, especially at such a young age.

I started to act like a completely different person and carried so much guilt around with me that I felt inferior to everyone else.

One part of being involved in the church was praying for a 'godly husband' to lead me in the way of God. When I was 17, I met a boy from a 'good' Christian family. He was a boy who I could see a future with — well, a boy who I *wanted* to see a future with. We dated for a year, and then as soon as I finished high school, BAM, I was engaged to be married. My older sister had married very young, as had a lot of people who I looked up to in the church, so I REALLY had the desire to do that. To get married young would mean I had it all 'sorted out'.

To tell you the truth, I was SHIT scared. I was finally the person I'd always wanted to be, but deep down I didn't know if I was making the right decision. Things started to take a rough turn for me. I became unmotivated and put on a lot of weight. I was afraid of seeing anyone and cried before going to events because of the way I looked. It was difficult to even have a shower. I remember having a phone conversation with one of my friends, who was a nurse. I told her that I hated going out, hated even getting out of bed or doing my hair and makeup.

She used the word 'depression' and my stomach dropped.

How had I got here? I used to be fairly confident, to love myself, and now the person I was looking at in the mirror was no longer me. A lot of the time in church felt like a blur. I had people-pleased for so long that I no longer recognised myself, my values or who I was deep down. I started to question everything. I went out with my old school friends a month before my wedding, drank a little too much and broke down to them. I expressed that I didn't know if marriage was the right choice. Had I made the right decisions in life? I felt that by following and chasing this 'I wish' life, I had become completely lost — more lost than ever before.

In my teens, I was constantly being pulled between a normal teenage life and a religious one.

On my wedding day, I was petrified. I knew I wasn't being my true self, but I couldn't disappoint these people. I knew that I was just postponing the problems, but I didn't want to hurt anyone. So I was content with just hurting myself.

Three months passed and the problems I'd been hiding started rising to the surface. I realised I was no longer myself: I didn't know who I had become.

My emotional health started to deteriorate; I began lashing out and experiencing daily panic attacks. I was questioning everything: what had I done? I told my partner that I needed to move out and sort myself out. I told him that I needed a break. But things got worse. Once people started to find out what I was thinking of doing, they started to call me. They started to abuse me. They started to try to dictate my decisions and tear me down for trying to find myself. Friends, family members, even people who didn't know me were making judgements about me and trying to persuade me to think and feel a different way. Gossip was rampant and suddenly I was hated by the majority of my community. It felt like all the walls of my life were caving in and I had nowhere to go, no one to turn to.

One night, I drank two bottles of wine in an hour all by myself. I played depressing music as loud as I could and found myself in the bath with a knife in my hand. Tears were streaming down my face as I placed the knife on my wrists. But something stopped me. This little voice in my head that I hadn't heard for a long time said, *You are strong. You are worthy. You are important. You can get through this.* I dropped the knife, got out of the bath and cried myself to sleep.

The next day, I made the decision that I was no longer going to live for other people.

I was going to start making my own choices for the sake of ME — to make myself happy, something I had not done for a long time. I broke off the marriage, moved out and started the next chapter. I enrolled in university and met some new friends. However, the whole event still haunted me. Every day, every minute.

The first year after ending my marriage was so rough, I don't think I was actually trying to love myself at all. I replayed the words everyone had said to me over and over again and believed that they were true: I had internalised them. My whole community had been ripped away so quickly and so I started to numb the pain. I started drinking all of the time and tried drugs to bury the horrible feelings deep down. I thought there was no way out and attempted suicide many times. How could I come back from this? How could I love myself? I struggled to see my worth. I struggled not to compare myself to others, to think about what other people were saying or thinking, and my mental health was super low. I had people-pleased for so long that I was disgusted with myself. I hated myself for ending a marriage that everyone was cheering for. I hated myself because everyone else hated me. I saw no way out of this self-loathing. I didn't know how to stop the repetitive negativity from outside sources and from myself.

I was broken and thought I could never be fixed. I had to find a way to move past all of the hurt, to forgive myself and move on. Someone I was close to suggested I see a professional counsellor and start posting on Instagram and YouTube to build my confidence back up again. 'Who cares about those people?' he used to say. 'They don't know you. This is YOUR time to be the you that you have always wanted to be: YOUR TRUE SELF.'

I started to challenge myself daily to try to REALLY love myself again. Some of the challenges were small and some were big, but over time they helped me get to the place that I am now. I started going to the gym, eating more healthily and putting myself out there. Christopher and I started dating and everything slowly came together. I focused on being creative and encouraging everyone to LOVE themselves and others ALWAYS.

This is where my self-love journey began, and it has been growing ever since.

Your self-love journey

This isn't a 'how to lose weight in 30 days' book, or a 'quote a day keeps the doctor away' book. This isn't a book that is so generic that it seems like it won't work for you. This is tailored FOR YOU and only you. You choose your journey, you choose your pace and you work out what works best for YOU. And to that end, I'm going to give you lots of ideas and opportunities in this book for finding that out, with exercises designed to help you realise more about yourself and what's important to you — your values and dreams, and the hopes you have for yourself in this world we live in.

This book has been created so that you can document your own realisations, dreams and thoughts, exploring your story in its pages. To get the most out of it, I encourage you to write, draw and scribble as you work through the activities. Use it as your own personal diary.

At the end of each chapter there are affirmations to help you achieve a more positive mindset. The way we speak to ourselves MATTERS. Every time you see an affirmation page, I want you to read the words out loud to yourself five times. You can repeat these affirmations any time you want.

I created this book to give you space to figure out why you should LOVE every inch of yourself. That's why I've included pictures of myself on some of the pages. It's meant as a celebration, not only of our physical bodies (which we should always celebrate) but of our inner selves, too. And don't miss the resources for healing at the back of the book, with suggestions for experts and rituals to help support you on your journey.

It's time to ground yourself. To come back to who you truly are and open up to your potential. It's time to take your power back in a world that tells you that you are not enough. Join me as we speak our truths and dig deep down to discover who we are.

Ariella Nyssa xx

After my divorce: I was faking a smile but on the inside I was broken.

1
—

Love your

INNER
CHILD

This chapter touches on experiences and memories from childhood. If you feel you may be triggered, please skip ahead.

I have always dreamed of a day when I would finally wake up and see myself as something greater. When I was a child, I wholeheartedly dreamed up an extravagant life for myself: I believed I could truly accomplish whatever I wanted to. I loved my body, I loved what I looked like and I loved my unique personality.

When we are kids we don't really think about external aspects of the world. We are so focused on having fun — being a kid — and most people would probably say they miss those days. They miss being a kid because that was when they weren't torn down by a world they didn't really understand. I think this is where we all get stuck.

This transition from being in the present moment all of the time — having fun and not overthinking the way we act or what we look like — to restricting aspects of ourselves to fit into the societal mould is different for everyone.

> There comes a time when we must 'grow up'. But what is growing up? Really sit and think about it.

When I think about growing up, I think about all of the rules society has placed upon us in every aspect of life. I think about how much I miss doing things simply because I wanted to, or not caring about others' opinions. Why can't we do that as adults? How have the negative attitudes of the world shifted our perspective on who we are?

Humans are amazing creatures. We have more than 6000 thoughts every single day. Our brains are intricately created and our consciousness is so incredible that we analyse situations, store core memories and instil a sense of who we are — all in that beautiful thinking and feeling organ.

So how have we lost a sense of worth along the way? If we are such incredible creatures, where have we gone wrong? When does it all change for us?

As you read in the introduction, a lot of my childhood and young adulthood was swept up in religion, which gave me a set of beliefs that coloured the way I saw the world. Although I no longer have the same beliefs, I often ponder about what humans are and how we got here. Here's a glimpse of the way I look at it now.

Visualise yourself in the moment before you are born: you are perfect and intricately designed. Your body — your Earthly dwelling — has the elements to survive, to live. You have organs that keep you alive, you have physical features that are designed to protect you from danger and you have a unique consciousness, unlike any other animal on the planet. In this state, you haven't 'become' anything yet: for the most part you are a blank canvas. You haven't formed relationships, values or goals, nor have you experienced anything that may colour the way you see yourself and your life.

Now imagine your parents holding you for the first time. As soon as you are born, structures are starting to develop. You are no longer a blank canvas, from the very first moments of your life. First your parents' experiences and personalities come into play. Each day you spend with them, you learn from them, you listen to them and now your blank canvas is no longer blank.

Your parents may start you off by placing a blue spot on your canvas and then their friends and communities may add a green spot and so on. As you grow up, more people come into your life to add to your blank canvas and, by the age of ten, your artwork is looking very chaotic. You're probably thinking, *Wow, ten is so young! A mere ten years on this Earth and already my canvas is almost full.*

We all have different childhoods — even siblings and people from the same families, communities and circles. Our individual experiences, no matter how similar they may seem, add different elements to our canvases, which means each of us is unique, even by the age of ten.

Your canvas is a unique artwork that reflects the people you have encountered, the things you were taught and the environments that you have been in. Some canvases are full of bright colours; maybe your life so far has allowed you to be who you truly are, with many positive experiences. A lot of us have fond memories of being a kid: making up imaginary games or friends, dancing, learning and growing. Everything in the world is new and fresh, and we saw the beauty in everything because we were seeing it for the very first time. Other canvases are darker and moodier, because some childhood experiences can be very negative.

We tend to think that certain events are 'normal' or that we had a 'normal childhood', but as the canvas analogy shows us, this is not the case.

> There is no such thing as 'normal' because our artworks are all made up of entirely different colours. We are all different.

Your childhood canvas

Here is a blank canvas. I want you to map out in different colours the elements of your childhood that you can remember. You can draw whatever you want. Maybe you want to scribble, maybe you want to draw something that reflects the different parts of your life before you were ten years old. I want you to dig deep to remember things that were said to you, things that were done or even life situations that had a huge impact on you. This is YOUR canvas. My canvas looks a little something like this:

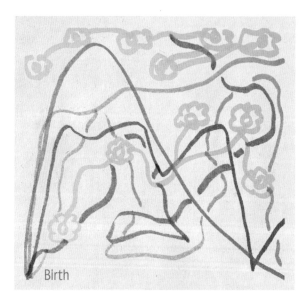

Birth

My canvas

♥ Parents
♥ **Community**
♥ Religion
♥ Relationships
♥ **School**
♥ Values

DARK AND LIGHT

Are there memories of your childhood or aspects of yourself that you try to push away? It's common to try to suppress certain memories and experiences out of fear or embarrassment. But the thing is, they are a HUGE part of who we are. And as much as we try to hide these parts of ourselves, they subconsciously affect our self-image and sense of self-worth, which affects our everyday realities. When we try to suppress these memories, we can feel like we are failures, that we are unloved or we are not worthy of the lives we really want to live.

These questions are to help integrate elements of your unconscious mind into your conscious experience. It's about acknowledging that the darker aspects of ourselves, the darker emotions, are just as important as the positive ones, so we can express ourselves in our entirety. (Remember when I said self-love was hard?) Answer these questions as honestly as you can.

Do you trust yourself? Why or why not? _____

_____

_____

_____

What emotions do you struggle with? Why? _____

_____

_____

_____

_____

What lies do you tell yourself about things from your past?

_____

_____

_____

What does 'embarrassment' mean to you? What do you feel
embarrassed about from your childhood? _____

_____

_____

_____

If you really loved yourself, what would your life look like? What are
the things that you would remove? _____

_____

_____

_____

_____

Think about an argument or conflict in your childhood. What made
you feel negative emotions in this situation? _____

_____

_____

_____

_____

_____

Dear inner child ...

Write a letter to your inner child about self-love and how strong you are.
First write a letter from your younger point of view to your adult self, using
your non-dominant hand. Then write a reply from your adult self using your
dominant hand. Writing with your non-dominant hand is childlike, while
writing with your dominant hand reflects your adult self.

Dear adult me,

_____

_____

_____

_____

_____

_____

_____

_____

_____

_____

_____

_____

_____

_____

_____

_____

_____

Love, young me

Dear young me, _____

_____
_____
_____
_____
_____
_____
_____
_____
_____
_____
_____
_____
_____
_____
_____
_____
_____
_____
_____
_____
_____
_____
_____

Love, adult me

TRIGGER WORDS

For a lot of my life, people have called me 'sensitive' or 'dramatic'. Why do other people's negative opinions or words get into our heads and affect the way we perceive ourselves? And how can we regulate our emotions when this happens?

Many things get placed upon us by other people while we are growing up. We may have been called names or had a situation arise that made us feel inadequate. When we have been hurt by others, we tend to dwell on our hurt feelings, on the way we felt in that exact moment. We may build walls out of hurt to protect ourselves, which makes it really hard to forgive others. But for now, let's focus on the fact that this also makes it hard to forgive OURSELVES. To forgive ourselves for feeling embarrassed, fearful or hurt. These feelings are also a part of us, and these situations and experiences are NOTHING to be ashamed of. They are part of growing, of learning, of what has shaped us. They are part of who we are.

Imagine another person saying the words below to you. Which would make you feel upset? Circle those words.

fat BORING *sensitive* emotional DRAMATIC ugly liar *grumpy*

MOODY touchy *angry* pessimistic ARROGANT big-headed vain

cynical overly critical INCONSIDERATE impolite defensive *cruel*

CONFRONTATIONAL *possessive* untrustworthy SECRETIVE jealous

stubborn resentful weird SNEAKY deceitful *inflexible* narrow-minded

FUSSY unreliable *dumb* messy GULLIBLE careless weak-willed *clingy*

mean SELFISH annoying *loud* judgemental OPINIONATED obese

spindly lanky senile SAGGY crazy PICKY *overthinker* incompetent

bossy BITCHY skinny *overweight* RUDE dismissive

Add your own words

Now answer these questions, either here or in your journal:

Why do these words trigger you? _____
_____
_____

Are these words true? If yes, why do they affect you? If no, why are
you upset about them? _____
_____
_____

Reflect on each word you circled. Why is it a bad thing?
_____
_____

What experiences have you had that make these words triggers
for you? Think back to your childhood experiences.
_____
_____

What is perfect?

While I was growing up, I held on to any negative comments and experiences and buried them deep in my psyche. I didn't want anyone to know about them, and I didn't want to relive them in my own mind. Eventually, I started dreaming of being someone else entirely, building a 'fake' life in my own head of who I truly wanted to be. Here are some of the thoughts that started crossing my mind daily when I was as young as six:

* Wow she looks so happy. I wish I was her.

* She's so pretty. I wish I looked like her.

* I wish I had her family and friends.

* I wish all the boys liked me the way they like her.

* I wish I had a REAL best friend, like you see in the movies.

* Look at her relationship! I wish I had a boyfriend like that.

I wish, I wish, I wish, I wish, I wish . . .

I was always wishing I was someone else, the type of girl who stars in Disney movies and rom coms. The type of girl who is accepted in society. The type of girl whose life is PERFECT.

Looking back, I see now that this wish list was poisoned with comparison, extremely unhealthy and completely unattainable. Why did I think I needed to be these things, or look this certain way, to be loved?

What I thought 'perfect' meant

PERSONALITY TRAITS

kind
funny
patient
understanding
confident
liked by all
social
intelligent
cheerful
calm
ambitious
motivated
creative
disciplined
honest
friendly
easygoing

APPEARANCE

shiny hair
clear skin
small nose
big lips
pert boobs
small arms
flat stomach
size 6
healthy nails
tight butt
skinny legs

MISS PERFECT

I'll bet you also have your own mental image you are yearning to be EXACTLY like. Fill in the diagram opposite with every standard that you hold yourself to. Think about movies you have watched, social media feeds you follow and people you have met. What is your 'perfect' human?

Now answer these questions:

Have you ever met a 'perfect' human? _____

What makes your 'perfect' human different from anyone else's?

_____

_____

What experiences, social media feeds, movies and relationships have shaped your idea of 'perfect'? _____

_____

_____

What would your life be like if you were the 'perfect' human?

_____

_____

_____

We are constantly striving to be perfect, but who decides what perfect is? There's a saying: 'Beauty is in the eye of the beholder'. *You* decide what is beautiful and what isn't. So stop picking yourself apart and criticising the way you look. *You* are the only one who decides your worth and your beauty. There are more than seven billion people on this planet and no two of us are exactly the same. So why do we all try to be that way?

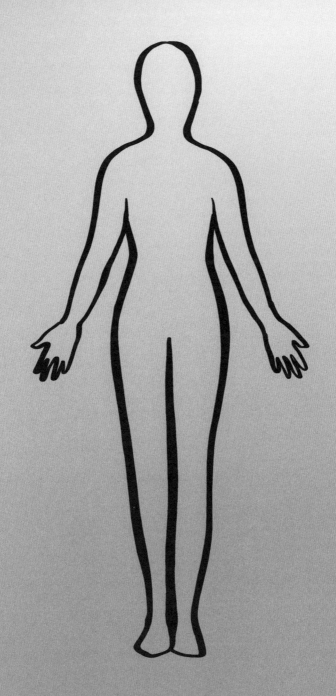

WHAT DID YOU LOVE AS A CHILD?

Acknowledging suppressed memories and aspects of ourselves is so important to our self-love journey, but it's also important to focus on the positive things that make us who we are.

When I was a child, I loved being creative and making up games with my friends ('mermaids in the pool' was my all-time favourite). I was always striving to do my best at whatever I put my mind to. I definitely wasn't a natural-born dancer, but I tried dance classes and made up dances with my friends. My mum and dad listened to music from all decades, and I found a love for all kinds of music. I loved to sing and auditioned for musicals and ensembles at school, and even though I was scared I wasn't good enough, I was really good at trying. I also loved animals and being out in nature, seeing the beauty in everything around me. I loved trying new sports and learning things at school.

Draw or write down ten things from your childhood that are the building blocks of who you are today. It could be your love for music, books or technology. It could be your love of caring for others or your passion for social justice.

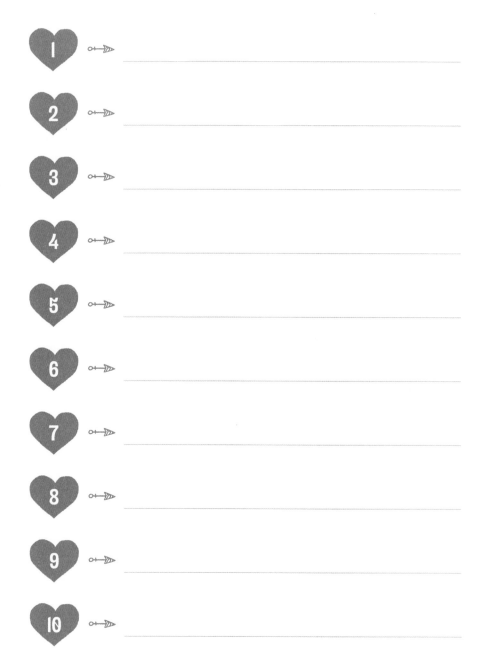

1. _____

2. _____

3. _____

4. _____

5. _____

6. _____

7. _____

8. _____

9. _____

10. _____

Your unique canvas, part 2

Look back at your childhood canvas on page 23. Has this chapter led you to any new realisations or feelings about your journey through childhood, and the inner child who still lives inside you? Thinking back on everything we have spoken about, use the blank canvas opposite to create a new version of your childhood canvas using colours, lines, shapes and drawings.

This is YOUR canvas. Your unique and beautiful canvas. There may be negatives and there may be positives, but this is your story. Your complicated, phenomenal story that is unique to you — no one else in the whole world has it. You are unlike any other. When you're done, take a photo of it and look back at it every day to remind yourself of how special your life really is; how special you are!

I know this was a hard chapter to start with and I am SO proud of you for getting this far. We have uncovered some truths about how life experiences and relationships have shaped you and how you perceive yourself. Childhood comes with so many trials and tribulations but it's also a time to experiment, grow and learn about our personalities and what we LOVE to do.

Inner child affirmations

♥ I believe you.

♥ Your emotions are valid.

♥ I choose to focus on healing all elements of my inner child.

♥ I acknowledge that my mental health is important
and I'm going to work on healing.

♥ I love you and I hear you.

♥ You didn't deserve this and I'm sorry.

♥ I forgive you.

♥ Thank you for never giving up and thank you for protecting me.

♥ You did your best and I'm proud of you.

Self-conquest
IS FAR BETTER
THAN THE
CONQUEST
OF OTHERS.

GAUTAMA BUDDHA, *DHAMMAPADA*

2

ACCEPT YOUR BODY

—all of it

This chapter touches on body image and eating disorders. If you feel you may be triggered, please skip ahead.

How do we go from being innocent children, loving who we are and not really thinking about the way we look, to comparing ourselves to others, dreading looking in the mirror, and feeling negatively about our bodies? One word: society.

If we really look at how society works, what do we see? We see marketing schemes, anything to make money. It's the driving force behind why we feel so bad about ourselves. We are encouraged to enrol in diet plans, sign up for gym memberships, buy cellulite-removal creams, do botox, buy clothes — all to change ourselves into whatever is currently deemed acceptable. For what? Honestly, think about why these companies do it. Is it because they truly believe your body isn't good enough? NO. It's because they want to make money, and that is evident through decades of changing beauty standards.

For much of human history, the epitome of female beauty was big boobs, big hips and a healthy body in general. A well-nourished body showed strength and fertility, and was appreciated for what it could do rather than what it looked like. It wasn't until the twentieth century that being 'thin' even entered society's standards. And ever since, beauty standards have been constantly changing, fuelled by marketing departments of the fashion and beauty industries. A flapper in the 1920s was told to be thin with no curves at all, while women in the 1940s and '50s were meant to have hourglass figures, with big breasts, small waists and curvy hips, à la Marilyn Monroe. In the 1960s and '70s, we went back to thin, curveless beauty (check out British supermodel Twiggy), then the 1980s shifted to bigger breasts and more athletic bodies, like Naomi Campbell and Cindy Crawford. The 1990s swung back to thin (Kate Moss), and now we're back to hourglass!

How can we keep up with something that is always changing? And why should we have to?

When I was about 14 years old, puberty hit me — and fast. I gained weight, grew enormous boobs (bigger than all my friends) and started getting increasingly emotional. Boys started to ask for sexual favours, and I began questioning who I was. I started to pick apart my growing body, and my self-image became solely dependent on my physical appearance. Social media was beginning to boom at this time, with MySpace, MSN, Facebook and then Tumblr my go-to websites. Girls started uploading photos of themselves, sucking in their stomachs and posing in that way that all of us insecure girls are guilty of. I was seeing models constantly on my feed and landed right back in that 'I wish' stage again. I wished I looked like them — oh, so badly I wished. *I need to be a size 6, that will make me pretty. That will make me happy.* I frantically searched for diets, exercises and all sorts of crazy regimes that promised to make me 'look like a Victoria's Secret model'.

I started different diets, but I was constantly changing them because they didn't work. I tried to starve myself and run around the block as many times as I could before vomiting. I tried to force myself to vomit after every meal, but didn't have the gag reflex for it. I was so unhappy with who I was … so I turned to boys. I tried to talk to as many boys as I could to feel accepted. To get compliments and feel 'pretty'. This was unsuccessful, another attempt at trying to find acceptance from others rather than going within for validation.

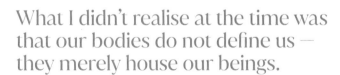

What I didn't realise at the time was that our bodies do not define us — they merely house our beings.

Read that again: *our bodies merely house our beings.* Our bodies protect us and carry us through life, but they are not all that we are.

What do I mean by this? Close your eyes and visualise your true self, the part of you that feels like *you.* Some people call this your soul, others your consciousness, essence or being. Maybe you'll imagine it as a glowing light, a feeling, or merely a thought in your brain. In whatever way feels natural, imagine this part of you being disconnected from your physical body. This is YOU. Say hello to YOU. Disconnecting from our physical bodies is an amazing way of realising that the body does not define who we are. We are more than what meets the eye.

What society seems to eliminate from its standards are the actual functions of the body, the intricate biological design of every human being. There is a unique and specific factory working within you every second of every day. If you think about the likelihood of you being created, let alone the trillions of cells that have formed you, it's an incomprehensible miracle. All of your cells have to coordinate into a specific and singular genetic code. Every cell is precise and complete. You have a nervous system, tissues, organs, cells and cell systems that build your body every day and repeat this throughout your whole life. You have trillions of neurons that make up your brain. You are able to self-heal. Each individual cell has its own function: you are a mastery of a biological hard drive. How incredible is that? Imagine a factory working 24/7 inside your body, making sure everything is working for YOU.

AND it doesn't stop there. The cherry on top of our biological build is that we have our own consciousness. Imagine your consciousness is like a wi-fi unit. It connects you to all of your cells and works through your physical apparatus. From the moment you are born you build and maintain a factory of neuroscience PLUS your biological machine. This machine lets you experience the world through your five senses: sight, smell, taste, hearing and touch.

Your consciousness allows you to drive this crazy and incredible machine; it allows you to live through your tangible and intangible experiences, giving duality to all aspects of life. Your trillions of neurons firing in trillions of different ways.

It's rare that we really think about the science behind the human body and mind. Maybe you are so caught up in society's expectations that you need a little nudge to remember how much of a miracle each and every one of us is. Aristotle and Plato both posed the question back in ancient Greece: HOW does the non-physical control the physical in human beings? That alone is MINDblowing.

Our personalities, our ideas, thoughts and experiences are a mystery, something to marvel at!

WE ARE MIRACLES. YOU ARE A MIRACLE. Until we know the science of our bodies we cannot become completely comfortable with them, with who we are. When I learned all of this, it absolutely blew my mind. It was like I knew all of this information deep down, but I'd never thought of myself in this way: that I am a miracle; that my body, my mind, my soul are miracles.

There's a one in 48 octillion chance of you even being here on this Earth. Of you even being born. Each of us has a completely different coding, singular and unique, unlike anyone else on the planet.

This chapter is a guide to learning to LOVE every inch of yourself. To love the beautiful housing for your being. To look after it and treat it with kindness. This may seem like a faraway dream for some of you, an impossible feat. But I'm here to tell you that it's not. I, too, have hated my body. I've dreaded looking in the mirror, going out and sometimes even getting out of bed because of how I've felt about my physical body. But the sooner we embrace our unique, individual and imperfect bodies, the sooner we will create an undying and unconditional love for the people within them.

What do you think you look like?

In most cases, our perception of our body is not reality. It can be formed through things like comments people have made and comparison with bodies in movies and social media. So let's start by getting a good idea of how you perceive your physical body.

How do you see your body? What do you think about it? Write some adjectives to describe your body. Is it healthy, skinny, fat, muscly, short, tall, weird, perfect, broken, healing, pretty, ugly, useless, helpful?

Now, draw a picture in the space below of the way you perceive yourself. Use as much detail as possible.

When you're done, take a photo of yourself using your phone or a camera.

Put your drawing and the photo side by side. Look at them carefully. Do you look the same in both? Was your drawing accurate? Really analyse them both. How are they similar or different?

YOUR BELLY

Often you only think of your belly in terms of its fat content and to compare it to other bodies. But your stomach has some serious storage capacity for food. Your digestive system absorbs vitamins from food, generates hormones and is your first line of defence for immunity. If you have a uterus, the skin of your belly allows your uterus to stretch and provide a home for a baby to grow. Amazing, isn't it?

Lie down in a quiet spot and put your hands on your belly. What do you feel? What do you hear? Take a minute to feel gratitude for everything your belly and stomach do for you.

Next, I want you to draw your belly below. But I want you to fill it with beautiful things. Rainbows, butterflies, sparkles, colours! Decorate it any way you want. Your belly is BEAUTIFUL.

Your legs

Everyone's legs are completely different. I got my legs from my dad's side of the family. I used to hate the way they looked because they don't have a lot of muscle. I wanted stick-thin legs, but my body just isn't built that way.

Let's simplify things. Legs can have strength. They give many of us the ability to go places and do things, and they carry us through the adventures of life. We may learn to walk, to dance, to live life through our beautiful legs. They are NOTHING to be ashamed of. A lot of people don't have the use of their legs, and that is BEAUTIFUL, too! Your legs share your own unique story, one in which they have helped you in so many other ways.

Stand or sit in front of a mirror and focus your attention on each part of your legs, starting from your toes and ending at your upper thighs. If you are able, tense and release each part as you focus on it, telling yourself:

'I love my toes because …'

'I love my feet because …'

and so on.

YOUR BREASTS AND BUTT

Breasts and butts have so many functions that we don't even think about. For many of us, our breasts can feed our precious babes, something that still blows my mind. It's incredible to think that milk comes out of those things! Our breasts are also protection for our beautiful internal organs. Our butts have their own purposes, not least giving us comfortable padding to sit on! Breasts and butts come in so many shapes and sizes, all unique, all beautiful.

Take a look at the breasts and butts shown opposite; all different shapes, all amazing. The absence of breasts is also a beautiful part of your body and your story. In the space below, draw your breasts and butt.

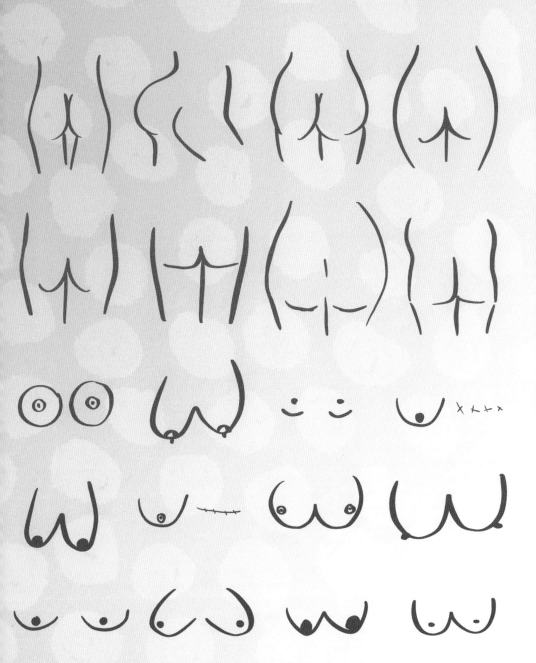

Your upper body

Your upper body houses your heart and lungs, internal organs that keep you alive. The muscles and bone structure of your upper body hold you up, protect you from danger and allow you to have a range of motion — whether yours is full or partial — to do things you love. Do you love to paint? Draw? Dance? Your upper body allows you to do all of that and more.

Stand or sit in front of a mirror so you can see yourself from the waist up. Wrap your arms around your upper body as far as they can reach and squeeze firmly. Tell yourself:

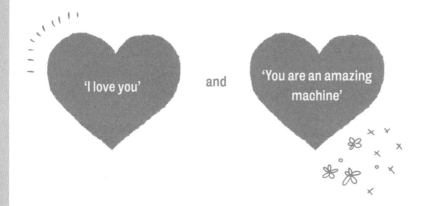

'I love you'   and   'You are an amazing machine'

CELLULITE, SCARS AND STRETCH MARKS

The marks on our bodies tell a story of who we are. I have always had cellulite and stretch marks, and I used to hate them because society told me they weren't 'beautiful' and didn't serve any positive purpose. But when I trace along each and every line, I realise that they tell a story. They tell the story of who I am and what I have been through in my life so far. They tell the story of my house, my physical house that has protected me, carried me and grown with me through life. Our marks are BEAUTIFUL and it's insane that the world tries to tell us any different.

Do you have any scars, stretch marks, cellulite or other marks on your body? If so, take some time to write about how you got them and what you have learned from that.

Your hands and feet

If you can, place your hand on the blank page opposite and use a pen to trace around it. (Don't worry if your fingertips go off the edge of the page!) Now, within the outline you've drawn, write down the things you can do with your hands; for example, draw, write, cook, knit, build things, eat, massage.

When you're done, lay your hand over the words you've written. Close your eyes and feel the gratitude rising off the page into your hand and flowing up your arm and through your body.

Use the lines below to write down the things you can do with your feet; for example, stand, walk, run, provide balance while you sit, wear cute shoes, drive a car, kick a football.

When you're done, take off your shoes and socks and find a nice soft patch of grass or smooth, bare earth. Place your feet on the ground, close your eyes and feel the gratitude for your feet rising up through your legs and flowing through your body.

Accept your body — all of it

YOUR HEAD AND FACE

Can you think of another person who has the exact same face as you? Probably not, unless you are an identical twin. Our faces carry our stories. The wrinkles and fine lines, the way our skin changes if we are dehydrated, the way our eyes change colour depending on what we are wearing or what we are doing. Our faces are INCREDIBLE. Many of us are able to speak and eat with our mouth, see with our eyes, smell with our nose and hear with our ears. And if we do not have one or more of those functions, our other senses will have heightened to adapt. Are you starting to see that our bodies live and breathe for us? They guide us and assist us in our own journeys. Each and every one of us.

What are your favourite things that your senses do for you? It could be your love for food, your ability to connect through touch or maybe your ability to see the world. For each of the senses, write down one thing you use it for that makes you happy.

Hearing: _____

Sight: _____

Smell: _____

Taste: _____

Touch: _____

Appreciate your body

Take a few minutes to answer the following questions:

What are some things you can think of that your body does for you? _____

_____

_____

_____

_____

What importance does society put on the types of things you wrote above, versus how your body looks? _____

_____

_____

_____

How has working through this chapter changed your perception of your body? _____

_____

_____

_____

_____

CREATE A HUMAN

Designing a human is complex! You need instructions, you need cells, you need structures within cells. No technology has *ever* come close to the complexity of human DNA. In Chapter 1, you described a 'perfect' human based on what your experiences, relationships and things you have seen have taught you about what's attractive and desirable. Before you look back at what you wrote or drew on page 33, let's do it again. But this time there's a catch: you have to design your perfect human including every single thing that you've learned while doing the activities in this chapter. It may seem like a simple task, but once you start you will see that the human body cannot be defined by just a few characteristics.

Redefine beauty

Sometimes it's hard to see our worth. When we start comparing ourselves to others, our whole idea of ourselves can get messed up in what society deems acceptable. But standards of beauty aren't the only things that have changed over the past decades — so has women's place in the world. It's time to take back our power and redefine beauty as way more than one narrow physical ideal, and about more than just our physical bodies.

Draw or write about some women who you think of as beautiful — not in the limited way society defines beauty, but how *you* define beauty. It can be yourself, friends or family members, a famous person, a stranger, even someone from your imagination. Everyone has their own story, their own body. See the beauty in us all. Don't worry about your drawing skills; this is for your eyes only.

Body affirmations

♥ Societal standards do NOT define me.

♥ Not everything I see in the media is true.

♥ I am not afraid of going against
society and being my truest self.

♥ I feel strong and confident in my body.

♥ My body is beautiful.

♥ I am grateful for what my body does for me.

♥ My body has overcome so much and is
working behind the scenes for me.

♥ My body deserves love and care.

♥ I accept and love my body.

♥ I am perfect and whole just the way I am.

♥ My body takes care of me.

ISN'T *every life,* ISN'T EVERY WORK BEAUTIFUL?

HERMANN HESSE,
SIDDHARTHA

3

GIVE YOURSELF
permission

This chapter touches on gender norms and memories of past trauma. If you feel you may be triggered, please skip ahead.

Society puts so much emphasis on gender. It starts the moment we are born — or even earlier, from the moment a baby's sex is revealed! Girls are given dolls and pretty pink bedrooms, with frilly pink dresses in the closet. Boys bed down in blue rooms with rugged play clothes and cars and trucks. We all know these stereotypes so well, and as we get older they become even more overwhelming.

Many people in Western cultures state that gender inequality is non-existent in this day and age. And it's true that women have been fighting for their rights since ancient Greece, and after centuries of struggle, including the marches and protests of more recent history, there has been huge progress. But today's young women and nonbinary people are still greatly affected by gender stereotypes and unequal societal standards. We still have to fight to prove that we are as strong and independent as men. We still aren't paid as much as men are for the same work. And we still have to prove that our worth isn't defined by our 'girly' characteristics and how big our boobs are.

Still today, women are placed in a confined box, expected to fit certain limited roles in the workplace, at home and in relationships. These 'secret rules' for how to be a woman are scattered throughout what we see in the media, in advertisements, modelled by our parents and teachers, and through thousands of years of ingrained sexist attitudes.

Have you ever asked yourself why women are still judged more on their physical appearance than men are?

Or why assertive women are slapped down as 'bitchy' and 'bossy', while assertive men are praised for being 'confident' and 'a real go-getter'? Why are girls taught to consider others' feelings and needs before their own, while boys are encouraged to be independent, bold and decisive? A lot of the ideas we form about ourselves are based on the roles and labels society appoints to us. People's opinions and judgements are hard to ignore and can have a huge impact on how we view ourselves.

Growing up in my church, where gender roles were extremely traditional, I changed parts of myself to fit the role of a woman. I got engaged right after high school because that's what I thought women were meant to do. On my wedding day, I was petrified. I knew I wasn't being true to myself by going through with it, but I couldn't hurt my fiancé or disappoint my community. Women didn't do that, right? As you've read, the pressure to fit into this 'box' of what a woman should be — to put others first, to not make any waves — didn't end well for me.

The patriarchal society we live in is overwhelming for so many of us — and I don't mean only women and nonbinary people. There are SO MANY harmful labels and limitations put on men, too. When we are all labelled through traditional gender roles, it can make us feel like we aren't enough, or like we have to live a certain way to fit in. But none of us can be confined by a box.

> We have to break down these labels and roles and start to define our true beings. We have to love who we are.

In ancient Egypt, the divine feminine and divine masculine were seen as dualistic. It was believed that ALL humans possessed attributes of both, and both genders were loved and adored equally. When I first heard this something clicked for me. Aren't we all a mix of feminine and masculine? Why can't we accept and love this mix of qualities in each of us, rather than having to be one or the other?

Let's strip ourselves of society's expectations, of ideologies, labels and fear of judgement. Let's be our complete and ethereal selves, giving ourselves permission to live this beautiful life in whatever way works best for us.

Recognise gender bias

Take a few minutes to write about gender. How do you feel about gender stereotypes? Have you experienced gender bias in your own life?

BREAK OUT OF THE BOX

Inside the box below, write down the societal constraints that you feel have had an impact on you or people around you. These can be gender roles, biases, stereotypes or any labels that you feel push each of us into a tiny box. The amazing thing about this activity is that ALL of us have a different box.

Now, grab a different coloured pen and draw over the top of all of these constraints. These things are NO LONGER going to hold you back. Embrace both the feminine and masculine in yourself. Breathe into the person you are and realise that you are SO much more than a label. You are so much more than a gender.

Call out people-pleasing

I read something on Instagram once that stopped me in my tracks. It said:

'People-pleasing is a form of manipulation'.

Read that again . . .

When I first read this, I felt angry. My guilty conscience yelled, 'Hey, that's not true!' It's difficult to be honest with ourselves. To be transparent and vulnerable. To admit our faults and flaws, and take steps to better ourselves. But when I really thought about it, it started to sink in. When we people-please, we are acting a certain way to make other people like us. To make other people happy *for our own benefit*.

Of course, it's more than okay to look after your loved ones and make people happy. But when it comes from a place of fear — fear of rejection, fear of failure, fear of being alone, fear of not being who we're 'supposed' to be — we have to look inward at why we are doing the things we are doing. Fear can take over our lives, but remember that we have control. It's time to take back control and do things because we WANT to. To genuinely make people happy without putting ourselves last, and to live our lives fearlessly.

Do you people-please? Write down some of the ways you think you have people-pleased and put others' happiness above your own.

FACE THE FEAR

Giving yourself permission to live truthfully, without limiting yourself by society's labels or limitations, is exciting, but it can also be scary, especially if you've experienced disheartening rejection or traumatising confrontations. After I decided to leave my marriage and experienced rejection from my community, I shut down. I put walls up around myself because I was scared. I was scared of being myself and people not liking me. I was scared of being vulnerable and honest with myself.

This is how fear works. You go through an adrenaline-filled, anxiety-riddled event and, BOOM, your brain tells you to be fearful. You go into fight-or-flight mode and run for the hills, telling yourself, *I am never doing that again. I don't ever want to feel this bad.* Long after the experience, you can hold on to this fear in a place called the 'pain body' — a phrase coined by Eckhart Tolle in his book *The Power of Now*. The pain body is an accumulation of emotional trauma that remains in your subconscious and impacts a lot of what you do. Most of the time you don't deal with negative experiences and push them into your subconscious, but even though you aren't experiencing these things every day, they can still impact your self-worth and the decisions you make. The pain body thrives on fear and stops you living your best life.

Write down your answers to the following questions:

What fear has held you back from being your truest, most vulnerable self? _____

_____

_____

_____

What event does your 'pain body' hold on to? _____

_____

Who can you rely on to support you when the fear takes over?
Hint: the first person on the list is yourself. _____

_____

What steps can you think of that will help you release yourself
from this fear? _____

_____

Write a list of all the fears, labels and stereotypes you no longer
want to control you. Beside each one, write down one positive way
that you can face this fear.

* _____
* _____
* _____
* _____
* _____
* _____
* _____

We cannot let fear hold us back any longer. It's time to shake
off our fear LITERALLY. I mean it, shake it off! Right now!

Permission affirmations

♥ I let go of labels and stereotypes.

♥ I will live an authentic life and be true to myself.

♥ I let go of all fear that rules my life.

♥ Fear no longer serves me. I create my own reality.

♥ I am not afraid.

♥ I will follow my heart and live a life without
fear of the unknown.

Facing it —
ALWAYS
FACING IT —
THAT'S THE
WAY TO GET
THROUGH.

JOSEPH CONRAD,
TYPHOON

4

Makeover

YOUR MINDSET

When people talk about self-love, they usually feed us surface-level solutions. Go get your hair done! Take a bath! Think good thoughts! But how do we even begin to do this?

EVERYTHING we dislike about ourselves stems from our mind. We let our thoughts judge our experiences and our views on the world and ourselves, rarely delving into *why* we dislike certain things. For example, you might hate your stomach. You might have seen magazines endorsing weight-loss products to help you 'lose those extra kilograms' before summer. Or you may have seen a celebrity slammed for her new baby weight. We all bury messages like these deep in our psyches until they become part of our subconscious thought patterns. Then the negative self-talk starts, building and building until it becomes impossible to sit with our own thoughts.

After my divorce, I was ridiculed in my home town. The things I heard people say about me were horrible: that God hated me, that I was embarrassing, a monster. I locked myself in and stopped doing the things I loved. How could I believe in my self-worth when no one around me did? It's easy to say, 'Don't listen to them. You know who you are.' But when you hear things like this over and over, you start to believe them. I developed anxiety and depression. There were days when I sat alone on the bathroom floor crying and ultimately trying to hurt myself. I didn't think there was a way out.

To be honest, I STILL have days when I fall back into these old thought patterns. My mind plays over every bad word ever spoken to me or about me. When I first started dating my partner Christopher, I would constantly ask him, 'Am I a good person?' and 'Do I even deserve love?'

It was Christopher who suggested I should post more on social media as a way to stop caring so much about what people thought and focus on loving myself again. He wanted me to see what he sees and to build my confidence back up. But as I posted more, my old friends started to mock me on their own social media channels. It killed me that so many people hated me — that I was the laughing-stock of my small town — and I almost gave up. But every time I fell down, I got straight back up again and kept trying.

Then in 2020, when the COVID-19 outbreak hit, I was forced to isolate and sit with my mental health. My posts on social media had delved into my love for my physical body, but my inner wounds were still open and oozing through all parts of my life. I decided it was time to start the real journey of loving who I was from the inside out. It was time to make a change, to reset my mental health, which is what I'm still doing to this day and will be doing for the rest of my life. Now I look back on this entire phase of my life as a huge learning curve. I used to regret it, to wish that it had never happened, but I needed to be torn down so I could build myself back up to be who I truly am.

The hardest thing about change is not repeating the same choices we have always made. It's about changing perspective and releasing the negative self-talk that we had given power to before. Remember the chrysalis?

 Butterflies are beautiful and represent transformation, yes, but the fact is that we are *always* learning and *always* transforming.

To truly transform our minds, we must focus on *continual* growth. And although that can be a hard pill to swallow, it's also empowering.

Humans are messy. We make mistakes and will always make mistakes. But the journey is about THE JOURNEY, not the goal. As soon as I realised this, it released so much anger, hurt and rejection from my mind. Transformation is about getting back up, resetting your mind and learning to love yourself through the ups and downs. When we get stuck in a cycle of bad thoughts, it can be hard to see the positives, to get out of this toxic way of thinking. But I'm here to tell you it's possible to remove this toxicity from your mind and start to see your mistakes and choices in a different light.

Your amazing mind

We have already touched on how incredible the human body is, but I want you to understand the science of your brain to get a better idea of why it works the way it does. Our thoughts have an impact on our bodies, our relationships, our self-worth and our lives, but *we are not controlled by our thoughts*. In fact, our thoughts are the result of our past traumas as well as our future worries.

Remember when I said your body is a factory? Well, so is your mind. In his book *Breaking the Habit of Being Yourself,* Joe Dispenza says that your routines are based on the thoughts that you have about yourself, your past and your future. For example, if you work a nine-to-five job, you probably have a set routine for each part of the day. You wake up, check your phone, make breakfast, have a shower, get changed and go to work. Then you come home, check your phone, make dinner, watch TV and go to bed. Similarly, our thoughts also follow routines. And each and every day, they will be exactly the same unless we become aware of them.

> Our routines and thoughts are embedded in our subconscious, telling us the same things over and over, even when we don't realise it!

Your subconscious mind is like a huge library, storing every memory you have as well as the emotions associated with it. It is like the encyclopedia of YOU, feeding things up to your conscious mind. I think that is pretty unreal. Brian Tracy, a self-development author and motivational speaker, states in his blog post 'Subconscious Mind Power Explained' that 'The function of your subconscious mind is to *store and retrieve data*. Its job is to ensure that you respond exactly the way you are programmed. Your subconscious mind makes everything you say and do fit a pattern consistent with your self-concept.' Your memories and the emotions associated with those memories are always with you — which is why a lot of us struggle with the past and worry about the future. And if we let harmful thoughts stay in our subconscious, they can actually manifest into our lives and our bodies.

Our subconscious mind may seem a little bit scary, and it may seem like we can't remove or alter these memories and emotions once they have settled in. BUT it is possible — and life-changing — to shift them.

When we start to have toxic thoughts, we simply need to learn to *notice* them with our conscious minds, and then retrain our brains to shut down the negativity.

This is why positive affirmations work and have been known to completely rewire our brains. Once we can see the thought with our conscious mind, we are able to question what it is really saying. And as we start to question these negative thoughts and toxic patterns, we are then able to retrain our minds.

Visualise your subconscious mind as a garden, and your conscious mind as the farmer. Whatever the farmer (your conscious mind) puts into the garden will affect the way it grows. Let's say we start with an empty field. The farmer begins by choosing the seeds and planting them. While the seeds grow, the farmer must water them, feed them and look after them. They keep growing until the farmer must harvest them so that she can eat and nourish herself. Sometimes our farmer doesn't pick the best seeds for our garden. For days, months, years, these 'bad seeds' grow and then the harvest is not nourishing. The only way to reprogram our minds is to replenish the garden.

Now don't worry, I'm not going to leave you with this information and run. In this chapter, I'm going to show you EXACTLY how to change your mindset. And even though it takes a little while, even though it takes some determination, discipline and some major changes in your life, I promise that soon enough you will be living the life you have always dreamed of.

Living in the past and future

For so long, I was living in the past and the future. I would replay my negative memories and thoughts, and worry about bad things happening to me in the future. Most of us actually live in this state even though we don't realise it. We spend our days rehashing the past and fearing the future, and then wonder why we feel so horrible about ourselves.

Take a few minutes to write your answers to the questions below.

Are there events from your past that you replay over and over?
Are there some that come up every day? If so, write them down.

_____

_____

_____

_____

_____

_____

_____

_____

_____

_____

_____

Are there worries about the future that you experience often?
Are there any that come up every single day? Write these down.

WHAT IS YOUR FREQUENCY?

Everything is energy. In fact, if you look at your hand — or anything, for that matter — under a microscope, you will see it vibrate. We are constantly in a vibrational state, and the energy that we vibrate has an effect on the matter and energy around us.

The Abraham–Hicks Emotional Guidance Scale, on which this activity is based, is a list of emotions, ranging from low-frequency emotions to high-frequency ones. High-frequency emotions are feelings like joy, empowerment, love, freedom, passion, appreciation, positive expectation and belief, happiness, optimism, hopefulness, contentment and enthusiasm. As we move downwards on the scale, the frequency lowers and we feel worse, from boredom, pessimism, frustration, irritation, impatience, overwhelm, disappointment, doubt, worry, blame and discouragement to anger, revenge, hatred or rage, jealousy, insecurity, guilt and fear. According to the theory behind this scale, when we are in a higher emotional vibration, we are able to attract more of what we want into our lives. We are able to accept ourselves and to engage in self-love.

Where would you place yourself on the scale opposite, based on your current everyday life? Circle that part of the scale.

If you are sitting in a lower-frequency emotion, don't fret! The main thing here is to identify where you are sitting, so you can gradually reprogram your mind and feel better about yourself and your life.

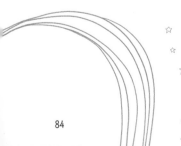

Ariella Nyssa's Self-love Bible

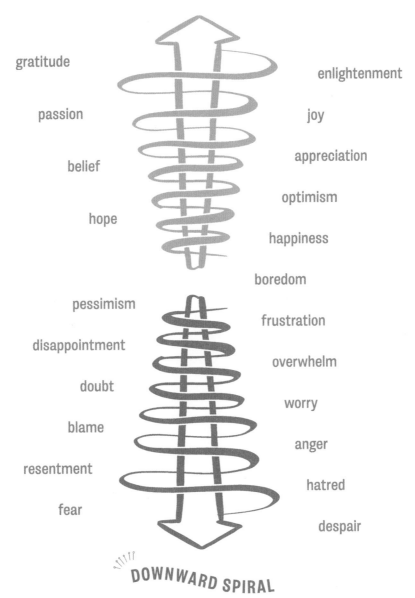

UPWARD SPIRAL

gratitude

enlightenment

passion

joy

belief

appreciation

optimism

hope

happiness

boredom

pessimism

frustration

disappointment

overwhelm

doubt

worry

blame

anger

resentment

hatred

fear

despair

DOWNWARD SPIRAL

When is it time to shift?

Shifting to a higher-frequency emotional state doesn't mean that you will never feel negative emotions, or that you need to be happy all the time. But if you are *always* in a negative vibrational energy, it can eventually be transferred to your subconscious and affect your body, mind, self-worth and even your relationships.

Let's take Amy, for example (a fictional character). Amy grew up being the 'popular' girl at school. She was used to getting anything she desired. She was healthy, well-liked, happy, social and talented. After school, Amy got a job as a receptionist. At work, Amy wasn't as popular as she had been at school. Her colleagues didn't like her and would harass and bully her. Amy tried to tell someone in management, but they laughed in her face and didn't listen. Amy's old school friends all moved away, met their partners and got married. Amy struggled to find time to go out into the dating world and spent most of her time at home by herself. As the years went on, Amy didn't even realise she was moving further down the vibrational scale. She did her day-to-day duties at work and had her set routines and distractions to keep her from thinking about the major changes in her life and the bullying she received at work. After five years, Amy was sitting in the lowest of frequencies, but she didn't even know it. She had been going through the motions for so long that she became complacent in the mundane and miserable life that she had fallen into. Amy hated her job, she didn't have supportive friends or family around her, her dating life was non-existent and she was getting bullied in her workplace. She forgot that happiness and contentment were even possible.

If you could soul-swap with Amy for a day, what about her life would you change to make her happier? _____

_____

_____

_____

_____

_____

_____

_____

_____

_____

_____

_____

_____

_____

_____

_____

_____

Maybe this story seems familiar? Are there aspects of your life that don't make you happy, but you do them anyway because they're a comfortable part of your routine? Maybe your inner critic tells you that you aren't worthy of doing what makes you truly happy. Maybe your inner critic has made you forget who you truly are and how valuable your life really is.

Deciding to change

When I was at university, I was studying to be a primary school teacher. Don't get me wrong — I LOVE kids and I always will — but my heart wasn't in it. I went through the motions because I had committed to the degree and was paying thousands of dollars for it. I was working in a job where I was getting bullied every day. I was too broken to stick up for myself, and I let the abuse go on for years. I felt like there was no way out, that I would feel like a failure if I quit. At the same time, I was constantly feeling guilty about my divorce, my old friendships and my old work. I felt upset and disappointed in myself, my mind on a constant loop of negative self-talk. I was stubborn and prideful yet unsure and discontented. I was all over the place. I didn't realise it at the time, but I was living in a low-frequency state.

But suddenly, I started to want to make changes in my life. I talked myself into making a YouTube channel and posting more on my Instagram. My photos started going viral and it quickly became my full-time job. I made a decision to defer my last year of uni — and I've never looked back.

> I hadn't realised, until all of these massive events happened, that I was just trailing through life.

I wasn't happy, and had been forcing myself to be okay with old decisions, decisions that were holding me back. It took years, but I'd finally decided it was time to change. To live a life I TRULY wanted to live. To let go of these negative emotions and do what I wanted to do. I wanted to love myself through and through.

WHAT'S HOLDING YOU BACK?

There are five main things that tend to restrict the love we have for ourselves and hold us back from unleashing our full potential. Take a few minutes to write about how you have done each of these things in your own life.

Comparison

Negative self-talk

Perfectionism

People-pleasing

Not looking after yourself

Breaking the negativity habit

To disrupt and transform negative thought patterns it's important to identify them. This is a difficult process because it forces us to sit with the negative self-talk and reflect on why it has become a part of our everyday lives.

For example, I get caught up in negative thoughts about social media. I start to look at the lives of others and wonder why my life doesn't look that way. I say things to myself like, 'You don't have the potential, you aren't good enough, you need to do better.' These negative thought patterns only make me go into a slump of self-doubt, which affects my work, my own posting on social media, my relationships and the trust and belief I have in myself.

When I was at my lowest point, I went to see my cousin Tamarin, a psychologist, intuitive and spiritual healer who runs EmpowHER Healing. She gave me this amazing activity to do whenever the negative self-talk becomes overwhelming, and she gave me permission to share it with you guys! It can be hard to believe in yourself when negative self-talk is rampant. But this activity will help you to see that these thoughts ... AREN'T TRUE.

List the negative thoughts that you have on a regular basis and how they make you feel. Put on a meditation track (you can find one online if you don't have a favourite) and sit with your thoughts. Let them wash in and out, and write them down on the next page. Next to each negative thought, I want you to write a positive belief that you have about yourself that will work to counteract this negative thought.

Ariella Nyssa's Self-love Bible

Negative thoughts	Positive beliefs

e.g. I just have bad luck all the time $\longrightarrow$ e.g. Good things can happen to me

BEING MORE PRESENT

Now let's make over your mindset with small shifts to break your routines and thought patterns and start living more in the present. Look at the list of thoughts you wrote down on pages 82–83 and, for each one, ask yourself:

✳ Is this under my control? Is there anything I can do about it? For example, is this thought nudging me to make amends with someone, or do something I've been putting off?

✳ Will this matter to me in five years' time?

✳ Is this thought helpful to me in any way, or just harmful?

Spend a few minutes journalling your answers on the lines below.

Now ask yourself: what are some small, easy things I can do to shift these thought patterns? If a thought is harmful and has nothing to offer but pain, what simple things can you do to break your routine and get past it? For example, doing positive affirmations or journalling. If a thought is helpful and urging you to action, what steps can you take? For example, if you're worried about having enough money, can you start saving a little each week?

List five things you can do to break your routine or shift your frequency when a harmful thought about the past or future comes up. Each morning, choose a few of these to work on.

1. _____

2. _____

3. _____

4. _____

5. _____

List five things you can do to take action on a helpful thought or worry about the past or future, such as forgiving yourself for a past mistake, or putting twenty dollars a week into a savings account.

1. _____

2. _____

3. _____

4. _____

5. _____

Shifting your mindset isn't a click-of-the-fingers thing; it might take weeks, months or even years. But self-love is a journey, and I know that you are ready and strong enough to embark on it.

Mindset affirmations

♥ I love myself and all of my being.

♥ How I feel matters.

♥ I choose to forgive myself and let go of emotions that no longer serve me.

♥ I am strong.

♥ I deserve happiness and to feel loved.

♥ I can reach all of my goals and am deserving of everything that I want.

♥ I am proud of myself for what I have achieved.

♥ Life's possibilities are endless.

THE MIND
IS ITS
own place,
AND IN ITSELF
CAN MAKE A
HEAV'N OF HELL,
A HELL
OF HEAV'N.

JOHN MILTON, *PARADISE LOST*

5

VALUE YOUR
uniqueness

I t's so easy to get caught up in competition and comparison. It may be with family members, friends or even people on social media. Maybe you run into someone at the grocery store and they start chatting about how amazing their life is, and you start comparing yourself. Or you're scrolling on social media and it seems everyone else is achieving more, moving forward faster, loving their lives. Before you know it, your mind is in an endless loop of negative self-talk, blasting yourself for any perceived flaw or mistake. You double down to work harder or look better, thinking that will help you compete. You put your true needs and wants aside and focus on pleasing others, trying to be who they (or society) think you *should* be.

But the fact is that no one lives the same life.

Run your own race instead of focusing on what others are doing, even if that means unfollowing people on social media who don't make you feel good, or distancing yourself from people when you find yourself starting to compare. Give yourself time to step back and set boundaries. Remember that social media is a highlights reel; people only share the good things in their lives.

You never see anyone's whole story, and they don't see the whole of yours!

In this chapter, we're going to create some personal affirmations for you to start moving away from comparison, negative self-talk, perfectionism and other common destroyers of self-love.

This information may seem overwhelming, but if you work on taking small steps to reprogram your thinking, you won't regret it. Your mind is an amazing neurological miracle! Don't let past trauma and self-sabotage be at the forefront: you are the creator of your reality. Let go of toxic habits such as perfectionism, people-pleasing and comparing yourself to others, and start to value the unique, one-of-a-kind person you are right now.

You don't have to keep waiting for something to happen to love yourself. Everything is already inside you just waiting to come to the surface.

The comparison trap

When you think of other people in your social circle or on social media, how do you feel you compare? Take a few minutes to write down your thoughts.

_____

_____

_____

_____

_____

_____

Let's create some affirmations that you can tell yourself whenever you start falling into the comparison trap. What can you remind yourself whenever you start comparing yourself to others? For example:

✳ I am individual and unique.

✳ I am enough.

✳ _____

✳ _____

✳ _____

✳ _____

✳ _____

NEGATIVE SELF-TALK

Negative self-talk has a huge impact on your self-worth. We can sometimes let these thoughts build up in our subconscious until we hate ourselves. But it's important to challenge your negative beliefs about yourself, forgive yourself for whatever you regret in the past and reprogram your way of thinking. (We'll talk more about how to forgive yourself in Chapter 7.)

What negative self-talk do you engage in?

_____
_____
_____
_____
_____
_____

Let's create some affirmations to start defusing your negative self-talk. What can you tell yourself daily to stop these negative beliefs? For example:

✳ I feel my anxiety and my emotions.

✳ Thank you for trying to protect me but I can take it from here.

✳ My negative thoughts are not real. I am loved.

✳ _____
✳ _____
✳ _____
✳ _____

Perfectionism

Perfection is something we all wish we could achieve. But none of us are perfect; in fact, *all* humans are imperfect. It's so important to set realistic expectations for yourself. You also have to be okay with failure. If we didn't go through bad things, or fail, we wouldn't learn new things, push ourselves, have empathy for others or be able to enjoy the good stuff! We just have to get back up and try again. Don't sweat the small stuff and try to embrace imperfection.

How is perfectionism a part of your life? What does 'perfect' mean to you?

_____

_____

_____

_____

Let's create affirmations to help you let go of perfectionism. What can you say to yourself whenever you find yourself trying to be perfect? For example:

✳ Perfect does not exist.

✳ I am worthy and I am content with who I am.

✳ _____

✳ _____

✳ _____

✳ _____

PEOPLE-PLEASING

Everyone people-pleases in one way or another, but it's something we have to remove from our lives to be comfortable with who we are. The difference between a caring person and a people-pleaser is whether we do things out of obligation, or because we are scared people won't like us if we don't. The truth is, we are never going to please everyone. Disagreements and conflicts are okay. It's fine to be different! We need to be a little bit selfish sometimes, to set boundaries and learn how to say no. It's time you start living for *you*!

How do you people-please? Can you think of three recent examples?

1. _____

_____

2. _____

_____

3. _____

_____

Let's create affirmations for when you start people-pleasing. For example:

✳ **Not everyone will like me, but all that matters is that I love me.**

✳ I'm a kind, caring person, but I uphold boundaries for myself.

✳ _____

✳ _____

✳ _____

Value yourself

You need to look after YOU. Your body and brain can't function properly without sleep, water, nutritious food and exercise. And you also won't thrive without fulfilling relationships, connection, a sense of belonging and a kind relationship with yourself. Start to look after yourself and you will see such a difference in your everyday life.

What are some ways you don't look after yourself?

_____

_____

_____

_____

_____

_____

_____

_____

_____

Let's create a few affirmations to remind yourself daily to look after yourself. Why do you deserve to love your body and mind? For example:

✳ I deserve love from me.

✳ My body and mind deserve to be taken care of.

✳ _____

✳ _____

✳ _____

✳ _____

Uniqueness affirmations

♥ The world wouldn't be the same without me.
I am worthy and divine.

♥ No-one can fulfil my divine mission in the world but me.

♥ I truly know who I am.

♥ I am individual, unique and unlike anyone else.

♥ I love and appreciate my own blessed uniqueness.

HAPPINESS DEPENDS MORE UPON THE *internal frame* OF A PERSON'S OWN MIND — THAN ON THE EXTERNALS IN THE WORLD.

GEORGE WASHINGTON

6

Let go
AND LET
FLOW

Okay, it's time to transform your consciousness. We have spoken about our bodies (biological machines) and our brains (neurological masterpieces), and now it's time to delve into consciousness and how it sits in the driver's seat of our brains and bodies.

When I started to learn about consciousness, it baffled me. And to this day, no one knows why humans have consciousness or where it comes from. Consciousness is the ability to experience the world around us, it's how we process information through our senses and our genetic makeup and previous life experiences and spark an emotional response. A simple example of this is eating food. Your tongue and tastebuds send information to your brain and you experience either a positive, negative or neutral emotional response. Let's say your favourite food is ice cream. You take your first bite or lick of ice cream and automatically your brain sends electrical signals throughout your body that trigger a positive emotional response. Now let's say your best friend takes a bite of her ice cream. Her tongue and tastebuds also send information to her brain, also arousing receptors in her body. It tastes good BUT this friend was ridiculed for being overweight when she was younger. She has vivid memories of eating ice cream and being tormented by others. Her brain sends out messages that the ice cream tastes good; however, these messages are immediately interrupted by feelings of guilt and shame, maybe even disgust.

Our past experiences have an undeniable effect on the way our brains function and the emotions we feel. As we discussed in previous chapters, if we don't interrupt this cycle, we will continue to battle negative emotions for the rest of our lives. We will never enjoy a delicious ice cream! But there is hope.

There is a way to break this pattern of emotional responses that make us feel awful. It is living in the PRESENT.

It sounds so simple: living in the present. I mean, aren't we always living in the present? But a lot of us actually live in the past and the future without even knowing it. Are you kept awake at night because you keep replaying your past over and over again? Or do you find yourself worrying about the possibilities of the future? If this is you, you are on what I like to call 'anxiety autopilot'.

> The truth is, the past is over and future hasn't happened yet. The only thing that is real is right NOW.

One of the things that keeps us from living in the present is ego. Ego can be defined in a bunch of different ways, but here I am referring to that part of your inner being that is your identity, your likes and dislikes, your core values, even your name and where you're from. Ego thinks it is always right, and is stubborn with its beliefs and core values. Ego tells us who we *should* be. Initially, we create our own ego to form an identity, one we can use to cope with trauma and confusion and protect ourselves from reality. But to live in the ego is a restricting and rigid life, bound by the constructs of the identity you have created for yourself. For example, your ego acts as a defence mechanism that doesn't allow in any new ideas or judgements. Your ego can restrict your growth and keep you in comfortable ways of being, getting in the way of reaching your true potential. A lot of adults STILL haven't dealt with their egocentric selves and might never do so.

It's impossible to live in the present moment if you are living an egocentric life. It's impossible to have healthy conflict, to grow or to be completely content and happy. Egos hold us back from being able to emotionally regulate, to be positive even when things aren't looking great, to see the beauty in everything, to disagree with someone on a calm level. It's time we push our egos to the side and start living our truth: that we are imperfect beings who can experience so much in life. It's time to shed our egos and start living in the present moment.

Meet your ego

Ego work is a shift in our consciousness. It's about disallowing the 'I's in our lives, giving us the freedom to just be: to not be held down by anything; to identify as a being rather than everything we have ever achieved or told to ourselves. The ego lives in the subconscious, so we don't even realise that it's there most of the time.

When we argue with people, we think we are in the right and our 'I' statements come to the forefront of the argument. The fight isn't about the initial trigger anymore, but about our beliefs, values and attitudes. It becomes about the EGO.

Take a few minutes to answer the following questions:

Ego statements start with 'I' and 'my'. What are some things your ego tells you about your identity?

_____

_____

_____

_____

Describe an event or situation when your ego came to the forefront.

_____

_____

_____

_____

HOW DOES EGO HOLD YOU BACK?

When you aren't feeling great about yourself, your ego tends to overcompensate. Look at the phrases below and circle the ones that most apply to you. Have you done these things before?

JUDGE OTHERS

HAVE STRONG EMOTIONS

MOCK OTHERS

FEEL DEFENSIVE

HAVE OBSESSIVE THOUGHTS

ACT COMPETITIVELY

COMPARE MYSELF TO OTHERS

SHOW FALSE CONFIDENCE

REJECT OTHER PEOPLE'S BELIEFS

INSULT OTHERS

BE ARGUMENTATIVE

Continued >

Describe a conflict that has arisen from your ego being at the centre of your identity. How does your ego hold you back?

For example, a friend might have been hurt by something you said. You might not have meant to hurt them, but instead of apologising your ego takes over and you become defensive. If you can let your ego go, you can focus on resolving the conflict.

_____

_____

_____

_____

_____

_____

_____

It's completely okay to have done these things or felt this way. Self-reflection can be really hard sometimes. Ego work is about getting back to our true natures, our natural beings — as we were when we were children. Back then, life was just about living! It's also not about feeling guilty about these things or our egos. The ego was designed to protect us and to shield us from the hurt in the world. We don't want to remove it entirely, just to soften it. We want to teach the ego that it is not at the forefront of our lives all of the time. It's about teaching the ego to step to the side, accepting our egos as something separate from us.

What makes you feel enlightened?

When I am living in the present, I feel a sense of *being*. Have you ever seen a really beautiful sunrise or sunset? Or smiled in the moment and felt truly happy? THIS is being in the present. That enlightened feeling that you get that makes you smile to yourself, that makes you appreciate your life and the people in it. For so long I hadn't felt like this, especially when I was going through my divorce and losing friends left, right and centre. But when I truly understood what it meant to live in the present moment and feel gratitude for what was in my life, these feelings became more and more frequent.

Write a list of things that you might feel enlightened by. It could be dancing at a festival to your favourite music, sitting around a campfire with your best friends, looking into the eyes of your soulmate or watching a sunset from a beautiful lookout. What helps you feel a sense of enlightenment?

*
*
*
*

QUIET YOUR MIND

For many years, my consciousness was taken over by negative self-talk and anxious thoughts. At one point, I realised I didn't like being by myself. I dreaded sitting alone with my thoughts. I used to call people when I was alone in the car, or listen to a podcast to keep my mind busy. I could never wake up from a sleep and just BE. I had to reach for my phone as quickly as I could and distract myself from my own thoughts. I still fall into this trap today — on autopilot, distracting myself from my mind and my feelings with technology. But how can we truly learn to be okay with being alone?

Being alone doesn't have to mean being lonely. In fact, to truly love oneself — and I mean *really* love oneself — we have to be okay with being alone. We have to be okay with whoever we are in this present time, warts and all. Humans are imperfect, messy creatures. That should be something that we adore, not something we try to get away from. No one ever has been perfect and no one ever will be perfect.

The present moment is all we have and it's all we NEED.

Meditation is a tool that has helped me so much. While I meditate, I am able to distinguish between the anxious thoughts and my consciousness, and eventually to completely be in the present moment. This was one of the imperative tools that I used to overcome my ego and live in the present. There is love in the world. Beautiful things are all around us. We just have to be present to see them.

How do I meditate? I like to picture my consciousness as a little person at the front of my brain. When I meditate, this little person is also meditating and floating in my brain. The deeper I go into meditation, the more my little person floats and glistens. This little person is the happiest when I am in a state of enlightenment, and meditation definitely helps me achieve this.

Focus on meditating for 20 minutes. Your ego might be resistant to this practice (in fact, mine is ALWAYS resistant) but you need to question the ego's intentions and work on opening yourself up to growth. If thoughts flood your mind and you can't quiet them, imagine your little person (consciousness) sitting by a beautiful river or lake. Every time a thought comes, grab a pebble and throw the thought-pebble into the lake! Keep coming back to this image whenever you feel like your thoughts are taking over.

Here are some steps to follow if you don't know where to begin. You can even play some meditation music as well.

1. Sit in a quiet, calm place with your back supported and your hands in your lap.

2. Take a few deep breaths, breathing in through your nose and out through your mouth.

3. Close your eyes and focus on your breath coming in and out, feeling your chest rise and fall.

4. If you'd like, start counting your breaths. Try to keep your thoughts focused on your breaths, or you can choose a word that you draw on when your mind starts wandering away.

5. You can do this for 10 minutes, 20 minutes, or as long as you like. Try to make it a daily activity.

Present moment affirmations

♥ I only live in the present moment.

♥ The past does not serve me.

♥ I detach from past experiences
and learn from negativity.

♥ I do not worry about the future.

♥ I feel enlightened and allow myself
to truly live every single day.

YOU MUST LIVE IN THE *present*, LAUNCH YOURSELF ON EVERY WAVE, FIND YOUR ETERNITY IN EACH MOMENT.

HENRY DAVID THOREAU

7

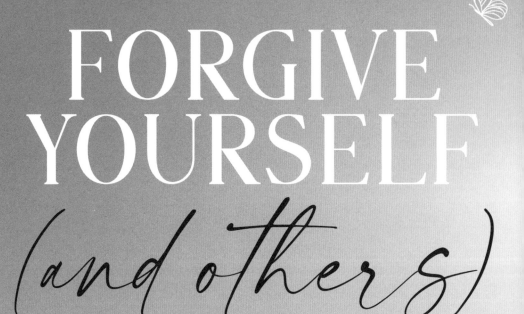

FORGIVE
YOURSELF

(and others)

TRIGGER
WARNING

This chapter touches on toxic relationships and anger. If you feel you may be triggered, please skip ahead.

Our emotions can sometimes run rampant. I know this from experience. When I was going through my divorce, I had no emotional regulation. I let other people's comments sway my opinions of myself. I cried 24/7, even over the smallest things. I was sensitive towards negative words about me and I let my past mistakes and failures define my self-worth.

Emotions are part of us and they aren't a bad thing, but when we let them take over, it can cause us to hold on to negativity and toxicity. A major part of self-reflection is being able to see mistakes that we have made from different perspectives. We can release our stubbornness and strive to do better next time.

All humans make mistakes — none of us are perfect — and it's vital to be able to reflect, forgive ourselves and move on.

For years, I held on to my mistakes. Because the divorce was my choice and I got so much backlash for it at the time, I blamed myself and that ultimately turned into self-hatred. I wasn't able to grow, learn or love myself at this time because the feelings of guilt were so strong. Without self-forgiveness, we can get stuck in a cycle that is toxic to our being and stops us from becoming the best versions of ourselves.

Negative emotions feel so uncomfortable, it's tempting to steer clear of them. We bury them deep down and stay in denial. But ignoring a problem doesn't mean it goes away. It stays in our subconscious, flooding to the surface in every aspect of our lives. There's so much power in claiming our mistakes and acknowledging that we are imperfect. If you have hurt someone, apologise — and that includes apologising to yourself, too. Being able to let down our walls and admit our wrongdoings is such a powerful practice. It takes strength and it allows us to fully let go of things that have happened in our lives so we can move on to the next chapter.

Resisting forgiveness leads to so many negative emotions: resentment, hatred, anger, sadness, fear, judgement. When someone hurts us, it causes an emotional and physical response. But to live in these low-frequency emotions (see page 84) is detrimental to our growth, to how we treat ourselves and others. For years after my divorce, I sat with the anger and it consumed me. I stopped trusting people and didn't let anyone in. I would be triggered by others' actions and constantly felt these negative emotions. But this did NOTHING for me or my growth. I was stunted. I had nightmares, I didn't want to sleep and I had to constantly distract myself. Holding on to this resentment wasn't affecting the other people; it was affecting *me*. I was overthinking everything, which had a huge effect on the chemical balance within my brain.

So often we wait for apologies. We feel like we need acknowledgement of the problem and an apology to move forward, but this just isn't true. To forgive someone is to let go of the emotions you have been holding on to for so long.

Forgiveness is for YOU. It's a release of everything that's limiting you from being your true self.

It's realising that those people didn't know better, that their actions are just a product of their experiences and their own reality. Humans make mistakes. We all do. Don't hold on to the resentment. Don't let it consume you any longer. You are deserving of peace and of love.

Forgive yourself

What do you need to forgive yourself for? Write a letter to yourself and forgive yourself for something you have held on to in your own life.

Dear me, _____

_____
_____
_____
_____
_____
_____
_____
_____
_____
_____
_____
_____
_____
_____
_____

Love, me

FORGIVE OTHERS

Who do you need to forgive and why? Write a letter to this person and FORGIVE THEM. Let it all go. This is a very emotional practice, so if you get upset as you do this, know that it's completely okay. Your feelings and emotions are valid, but the negativity associated with your unforgiveness does not serve you any longer.

Dear _ _ _ _ _ _ _ _ _ _ _ , _____

_____

_____

_____

_____

_____

_____

_____

_____

_____

_____

_____

_____

Love, me

What does forgiveness look like to you?

This sounds broad but the amazing thing is that every single one of you will draw this differently. Maybe forgiveness feels like weights being lifted off your body. Maybe it feels like walking into the most beautiful garden you have ever seen. Maybe it looks like your favourite colours entering your body and negative colours being released. Draw whatever comes to your mind.

LEARNING THROUGH FORGIVENESS

What can you learn from your previous experiences? What have you learned from the things you need to forgive yourself for? Write these below.

Forgiveness affirmations

♥ I forgive myself.

♥ I cut the energetic ties with people who have
hurt me in the past. I forgive them.

♥ I release anxiety, resentment, hatred
and guilt from my being.

♥ I trust that my forgiveness is for my best self.

♥ I do not understand people's actions,
but I understand that humans make mistakes.

THE WEAK CAN NEVER FORGIVE. FORGIVENESS IS AN ATTRIBUTE OF THE *strong.*

MOHANDAS K. GANDHI, *YOUNG INDIA*

8

Trust YOURSELF

The art of trusting yourself: again, it seems like a simple feat. But have you ever been umming and ahhing about a situation in your life, unable to decide? Maybe you have a gut feeling but need a bit of a push to get yourself over the line. You ask a million questions to multiple people in your life, wanting to hear a certain answer in their advice.

A lot of the time we DON'T trust ourselves, instead seeking external validation or confirmation from outside sources. We might speak to six different people just to hear the answer that we already have in our heads. It feels good to hear someone say that our thoughts or feelings are valid. And, of course, it's okay to seek help and wisdom from others. But what's not okay is to *only* rely on other people, not trusting yourself to make the right decisions. How can anyone else make the decision for you?

The only person who really truly knows what's right for you is YOU.

Trusting ourselves is a reflection of how we feel about ourselves. When our self-worth is low and negative words fly around in our minds, we tend to talk down to our inner beings. We don't trust them or believe them, and our egos make up identities that don't allow us to grow or make decisions for ourselves. Or maybe you are the opposite, your ego at the forefront making decisions left, right and centre that may be hurting other people and ultimately hurting yourself.

Have you ever heard the test-taking trick that says you should always trust your first answer? The thinking is that your intuition and knowledge usually tell you the right answer in the first minute after reading the question. But sometimes we overthink things and change the answer. In relationships, our intuition works to protect us. Maybe you have been in a toxic relationship before and knew deep down in your gut that it was going to hurt you, but you stayed. Or maybe you have a gut feeling that one of your friends is gossiping about you behind your back, but you choose to ignore it. Why do we disregard our intuition in so many parts of our lives?

Intuition is a very real psychological process. It uses past life experiences, cues from our environment and the context of a specific situation to automatically and unconsciously calculate the outcome of that situation. There are 100 million neurons in your gut used to process stimuli. These neurons then send signals to your brain! This is also the case for your heart. Your brain then translates these neuron survival signals and, if emotions are triggered, your ego will resist, censor and even edit the information it receives in an attempt to protect itself.

Think of your intuition as actually coming from three brains: your head, your heart and your gut. Your head analyses and makes sense of information and data collected through your five senses. It interprets this data and fills your consciousness with rational evaluations of a specific situation. Your heart receives this data and sparks an emotional response based on your desires, passions, aspirations, regrets and disappointments. And lastly, if your analysis triggers a fearful emotional response, this is your gut being activated. Your gut feeling provides you with two options: succumb to the fear (flight) or push back (fight). Of course, if the gut is telling you to run away from danger, listen to it and run away! But if the gut is telling you not to wear a certain outfit because you're scared of others' opinions, then be courageous, go against the gut and wear what you want.

The three brains are vital in understanding and breaking down why we make decisions. I find that breaking down what seems to be a 'simple' emotional response allows us to perceive ourselves in a much better way. It allows us to understand the 'why' behind our emotions and we can draw on this in so many different parts of our lives.

Being able to trust your intuition stems from having a secure and confident relationship with YOURSELF.

It is about backing yourself and committing to your decision and your idea, no matter the external influences. When I was married, my gut feeling told me that I wasn't in love, that I was people-pleasing, that there was something more to love than what I had. It was no one's fault — not my husband's, not mine. It was simply that we weren't compatible, we weren't on the same vibrational frequency, we didn't align. Trusting my intuition and leaving that relationship led me to levels of achievement and happiness I didn't think were possible. Had I stayed just to please others, I would have never started my career, discovered my passion or, most importantly, met my best friend and now partner Christopher.

It's okay to trust yourself. You KNOW what makes you feel good and bad. You know what red flags look like. It's time to trust yourself.

Listen to your gut

Close your eyes and picture a deer in the wild. It's calm and eating in a forest. It hears one snap of a twig and suddenly stops eating. It may not see any danger, but it senses it and automatically runs. Now imagine if the deer did not run but stayed eating happily in the forest. And all of a sudden, BAM, a predator comes out of nowhere and attacks the deer.

Now think of a situation from your past when your gut sensed danger and you ignored it. Did you try to see good in a situation when, deep down, you knew it wasn't great for you? It's time to start trusting yourself, trusting that your experiences, knowledge, intelligence and intuition serve you. You are more than capable of making decisions that affect you positively.

Speak positive words to your gut that express your truths and will allow you to start believing more in yourself. Put your hand on your gut and say:

✳ I trust my intuition.

✳ My gut is here to protect me and to guide me.

✳ I trust myself.

✳ I am an open and clear channel.

✳ I am connected to my higher power.

✳ I trust the guidance that my intuition gives me.

✳ I am willing and open to listening to the inner words that protect me.

✳ I am moving into alignment with my higher self.

YOUR THREE BRAINS

Think of a situation from your past when you had to make a big decision. Remember the difficulty you had making the decision. What did each of your brains say? Write about the answers in the spaces below.

What was the decision you had to make? _____

_____

_____

_____

Head brain: this is your analytical brain. What did your head tell you? _____

_____

_____

_____

_____

_____

_____

Heart brain: this is your emotional brain. What did your heart tell you? _____

_____

_____

_____

_____

_____

_____

_____

Gut brain: this is your intuitive brain. What did your gut tell you?

_____

_____

_____

_____

_____

_____

What did you end up deciding? And what can you learn now from
how that decision turned out? _____

_____

_____

_____

_____

_____

_____

_____

_____

_____

4 steps to making decisions

Is there a decision you're struggling to make? Even when we feel like we are confused, our body often gives us a clue. Think about a tough decision you're facing (or one you faced in the past). For example, let's say you are thinking about buying a house but aren't sure if it's a risk you should take. Sit with each option and feel the emotions associated with it. Imagine *not* buying the house. Do you feel sad? Do you feel disappointed? Or maybe relieved? Now imagine buying the house. Do you feel excited? Inspired?

Here is a four-step process for making clearer and better decisions for yourself in any given situation. Use this guide whenever you are feeling confused or uneasy about your intuition. If you have a decision to make now, journal some thoughts below.

1. Breathe. Take a moment to reflect. Sometimes our reactions can be based on fear, low self-worth and emotional triggers. Take some deep breaths and sit with the decision-making process. Take the time to really listen to your intuition, or gut brain. What does it say?

2. Do some research, journal or speak to someone who wants the best for you. Most of the time, your intuition will tell you straight away what answer you are looking for, based on your own past experiences, memories and your true being. It's good to get advice sometimes, but make sure you sit with your intuition, too. Give yourself time to weigh up the options.

3. Remember to use all three brains and journal about what each one says:

   ✳ What does your head (analytical) brain say?

   ✳ What does your heart (emotional) brain say?

   ✳ What does your gut (intuitive) brain say?

4. Breathe again. Trust the process and make sure you are in a calm state before making any huge decisions.

Trust affirmations

♥ I believe and trust in myself.

♥ I trust my intuition.

♥ My gut feelings should never be ignored.

♥ I have nothing to fear.

♥ I trust my power to guide me on the right path.

♥ My security comes from within.

♥ I am thankful that my body tells me
when something isn't right.

♥ I trust myself.

SELF-TRUST IS THE FIRST *secret* OF SUCCESS.

RALPH WALDO EMERSON

9

FIND THINGS TO BE *Thankful* FOR

Practising gratitude, in basic terms, is finding the things you are thankful for in your life. These can be big or small things, but either way it's an incredible practice to help you feel enlightened and positive.

It sounds so simple to 'practise gratitude' or be thankful for the things in your life, but sometimes — when the world around us is crashing down or we are stuck in a negative way of thinking— it can be really hard. We all deal with different things in our lives. I want to be as sensitive as I can be with this topic because I know I have lived a privileged life. I was raised in a family that was not abusive, and I have never dealt with horrific trauma. I'm not a part of any marginalised group and I have always had food on the table. I know for many this is not the case, and it may not be as simple as saying 'be grateful for what you have'. Sometimes it's not as easy as reading a self-love guide and going on your way. Certainly, if you are struggling with issues that go beyond the scope of this book, please don't hesitate to reach out to some of the support services listed on pages 222–223.

I have two stones in my house that always remind me about gratitude. One of the stones I found when I was camping, and couldn't believe how perfect it looked. The other stone I found when I was on a walk and was peacefully watching the world: the birds, butterflies, trees and people around me. I brought the stones home to remind me of how I felt in these moments, and I keep one in the bathroom and one next to my bed. I found these stones on different days, at different times and in different locations, but at the time I found both of them, I was feeling so grateful. Both times, I was smiling from ear to ear, smelling the flowers as I walked and finding beauty in everything I saw. I felt gratitude for the world around me, and that I could immerse myself in nature. I chose to put these stones in my house, in places I am in often during the day, so every time I see them I am reminded of the beauty all around me and of the things I am grateful for in my life.

Everything has its own journey and its own amazing life. Take an ant, for example. You have probably seen a lot of ants in your life. Most times you probably saw the ant, made an observation that you just saw an ant and then went along with your day. But what if you sat down and watched that ant for a while? You would probably realise that this little ant is a being, with a life. It's on its own journey, doing what it can to survive. You might remember that ants are social insects that live in colonies ruled by a queen ant. You might remember that an ant can lift 20 times its body weight, and that there are more than ten thousand species of ants in the world. Ants aerate the soil, allowing oxygen and water to reach tree and plant roots. They also drag fruits and seeds around, which provide nutrients for the soil. Without ants, vegetation all around the world would suffer immensely. Remembering all of this might make you a little grateful for this ant. Grateful because without this ant, the human species would be greatly affected. This can be said for any living creature, plant or natural thing in this world. While I say it's the 'simple' things that we need to start being grateful for, you might notice that these 'simple' things aren't really that simple at all.

We are all connected: the universe, nature, animals, humans. Our energy is universal. We can get so caught up in social expectations, relationships and the 'man-made' world around us that we forget what it actually means to LIVE and BE. Your ego may tell you that you don't have time to just 'be' — you have a deadline to worry about, a photo you need to post, friends to see. But step away from those thoughts for a second and just be. Be in nature.

Look for the beauty. Look at the incredible world that we live in without all of the complicated stuff.

I swear to you that I used to hardly ever see butterflies, but ever since I started this gratitude practice, I see multiple butterflies every single day. And do you know why? Because I'm LOOKING for the beauty. I'm watching the world around me.

There are many things we can be grateful for. It could be a rainy Sunday, cuddled up with your loved ones. It could be dancing with your friends or singing your favourite song. We can choose to feel gratitude in every part of our lives, we just have to be present to experience these moments.

Flower of gratitude

Write one small thing that you are grateful for in each petal of the flower below. Once you have written them down you will see how many things you have to feel grateful for! Some suggestions to start you off: your family, friends, pets, house, food, the weather.

WHAT IS A LIFE WORTH LIVING?

Beauty doesn't have to be seen with your eyes. Think about the all of the things that make your life beautiful. It could be friends, a loving partner, your appreciation of good music or good food, your ability to be self-aware, or the health and safety of your loved ones. Everything is subjective to the person. Write about or draw what a 'beautiful' life looks like to you. Your 'beautiful' life is individual to you and that is so incredible! Don't forget to be grateful that there's nothing stopping you from truly loving yourself.

Make a beauty map

It's time to start looking for the beauty around you. On a walk, commuting to your job or sitting in a park or at the beach, put your phone away and just LOOK for the beauty. What can you see? When you see something, stop for five minutes. Really soak it in. Give it a smile and say hello (yes, even if it's a beautiful flower or plant). Smell it, touch it and give gratitude for it. This has become an essential practice in my everyday life.

When you get home, make a 'beauty map' of your journey in the space here, including the different things you saw.

FINDING GRATITUDE WHEN THINGS ARE HARD ♡

When life gets really difficult, it can be hard to see the good things. But everything in life can be treated as a lesson. Our past experiences don't have to hold us back from being happy or feeling loved. Below, write about a time when you felt helpless. Why did you feel this way? What stopped you from appreciating the beauty in everything around you and held you back?

Now let's flip the narrative. What did you learn from this experience?

Gratitude tokens

Find a few stones or shells to place in your home, so that when you see them you are reminded to be grateful. But there's a catch! You have to go outside to one of your favourite places and explore to find the stones or shells. Make sure you're allowed to remove them from wherever you are, then place them around your home where you will see them often.

Gratitude affirmations

💙 I am grateful for who I am.

💙 I am grateful for my journey.

💙 I am grateful for my friends, family and loved ones.

💙 I am grateful for the world, nature and
everything surrounding me.

💙 I am grateful that I am on the right path.

THEY SHOULD
Think
THEIR COARSE FOOD
SWEET; THEIR PLAIN
CLOTHES BEAUTIFUL;
THEIR POOR DWELLINGS
PLACES OF REST;
AND THEIR SIMPLE
WAYS SOURCES OF
ENJOYMENT.

LAO TSE, *TAO TE CHING*

10

SUPPORT YOURSELF WITH POSITIVE *relationships*

This chapter touches on past trauma and toxic relationships. If you feel you may be triggered, please skip ahead.

Humans are social beings. And although communication exists in most other species, there are very few that communicate in as complex a manner as we do. We use language and non-verbal communication to express emotion, to seek and provide information and to persuade. We can communicate verbally, physically and even with just a slight facial expression. Over millennia, the human neocortex — the part of our brains that drives higher brain functions such as decision-making, perception and language — has expanded greatly and is much larger than that of other species. When we are in social situations, the neocortex lights up and expands! Why am I going into the science behind communication? Because communication and conflict are ESSENTIAL to our lives as humans.

I bet you can think of a hundred positive interactions with both loved ones and strangers. So many of these experiences can shape who we are, our values and how we view the world around us. Our relationships teach us so much, adding different elements to those canvases of our lives. They say that eventually you begin to turn into the people you surround yourself with. When we are younger, we don't think of our friendships in this way. We meet our friends by accident through school, parents or in our neighbourhood and suddenly these people become huge parts of our lives.

Your tree of friendship

Just as our DNA and relationships connect us to a 'family tree', we can also think of a 'friendship tree', connecting us to those who have been at the centre of our lives at one point in time. This tree analogy is useful to show you the impact that negative and positive relationships have on your life. Sometimes it may feel as though a relationship or friendship can break us, but this tree will show you that sometimes it's a good thing to let the wind blow these friendships in the other direction, and that we can learn from every interaction we have.

In your friendship tree, the tree trunk is your stability: it's you. Deep beneath the tree trunk are its roots, holding up the trunk, sprouting new and amazing shoots and keeping the tree grounded. These roots are friendships that are everlasting and make a huge impact on your life. These may be childhood friends, siblings or people you have met later in life who you just know are going to stick around.

Although you can't see the roots, the tree will not survive without them. They provide the nutrients and structure to the tree from the inside out. They dig deep below the soil, and even if you don't see them, they are always there.

These are the friends who provide you with strength, comfort, support and love no matter what you are going through.

The values that I hold within the roots of my tree include loyalty, compassion and unconditional love. I'm sure you have your own values in your roots, too.

Then we move along to the branches. The branches symbolise friendships that are strong but can be broken. These friendships may look strong from the outside and may hold firm and strong for a fair while, but they aren't as dependable as they may seem.

The tree's leaves symbolise friendships that can easily go with one gust of wind or a change in season. They are useful for a while, providing nourishment and shade and other needs, but once their time is over, they turn brown and fall away. These are like the friendships that are conditional, that change depending on the choices you make or how they are feeling at the time. These are friends who take your energy for a time and then leave you bare.

Friendship is just like this tree. There are many friends who are in it for the long haul, people you can depend upon and who will be there forever. But just as easy as it is to make friendships, it's easy to lose some of them. We have all lost friends, and honestly that can be just as hard as going through a partnership breakup. It can feel like losing a part of yourself, with the attributes that you picked up through the relationship slipping away before your very eyes. But we must remember that we are all human. Humans are messy, emotional and sensitive. We take things personally; we feel rejection, and conflict can be a really hard thing to navigate through. And sometimes, our self-worth doesn't allow us to let the right people into our lives — or lets the wrong people in.

Relationships and the 'trauma-self'

As you read on pages 10–11, when I was 16, I went to a summer youth camp through my church and reconnected with people in that community. I made friends at church again, and had young people around me who completely supported me and seemed to want the best for me. It seemed like they really cared. These relationships started so positively, but I soon realised that this love and acceptance was conditional and toxic.

Sometimes if we haven't dealt with trauma within our own lives or have low self-esteem, we can create friendships with people who reflect our own traumas. I had felt rejected by boys and people outside of Christianity and was ready to 'belong' to a group, to have that feeling of validation. I had been yearning for so long to find people I really connected with, who shared similar interests and values, and I thought I had finally found them. I realise now that my 'trauma-self' was at the forefront of these relationships. That the struggles I'd had during my childhood had a lasting impact on what I accepted as friendships, and the extent to which I would let my so-called friends' opinions control my life.

A trauma-self is a subconscious state that develops from trauma that we have experienced throughout our lives and, since it is at the forefront of our subconscious, can make us more vulnerable to external influences. Our friendships and relationships are then established through the trauma-self. This is why many of our relationships reflect the internal noise of our subconscious thoughts. If you think of this in terms of my journey, my trauma-self was attracted to a sense of 'belonging' with a group of people who all seemed like they accepted and loved each other. Their closeness allowed me to feel like I, too, could be a part of their group and form strong relationships, which is what my trauma-self had always wanted and desired.

When I was involved in the church, I was adamant that these people were roots in my life because I had known them for so long. But I learned the hard way that their friendship was conditional. If I made a mistake, changed as a person, or started to live in a different way than they did, their love, support and loyalty would be withdrawn. Eventually, once I became fed up with feeling bad about myself, I started to cut ties with people who didn't want the best for me, who thought they could dictate my life and judge my choices. It was the best decision I've ever made.

Having trustworthy and loyal people around you is important in succeeding at anything you do in life. When we have people who constantly bring us down, belittle us and make us feel like we can't achieve anything, these thoughts WILL stay with us.

Who are the people who are feeding your soul, who are happy to watch you grow into the person you are supposed to be?

We all need to be surrounded by people who light up when we glow, who love us unconditionally and support us through thick and thin. Remember the friendship tree we discussed earlier? YOU deserve to have firm roots that ground you in who you are!

What defines relationships for you?

It's taken me a long time to figure out what a true friend is and what values I hold close when giving my energy to the people around me. What do the words 'friendship' and 'relationship' mean to you? What do they look like? Maybe your definition of relationships stems from the way your parents treated each other, or from watching your older sibling with their friends. Maybe it was based on movies or TV shows that you watched when you were young. Maybe it comes from past experiences with friends whose love for you was conditional.

Journal your answers to the following questions, being as honest as you can.

What has been your most defining relationship, other than with your family? _____

_____

_____

_____

_____

_____

_____

_____

_____

Have you ever felt like you don't belong in your friendship circle?

_____

_____

_____

_____

Have you ever cut a toxic person out of your life? How did you do it?

_____

_____

_____

_____

_____

_____

_____

Write about some relationships that you may have created while in your 'trauma-self'.

_____

_____

_____

_____

_____

_____

_____

_____

_____

5 FRIENDS

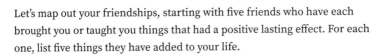

Let's map out your friendships, starting with five friends who have each brought you or taught you things that had a positive lasting effect. For each one, list five things they have added to your life.

Here are mine, as an example. Take a look and then draw your own.

Friend 1 ✳ How to unleash my humour and be silly ✳ How to be a leader
✳ Respect ✳ Kindness ✳ To be non-judgemental

Friend 2 ✳ Discipline ✳ Values ✳ Faith ✳ Boundaries
✳ To talk to about my feelings

Friend 3 ✳ To talk to other people ✳ To party ✳ To embrace my sexuality
✳ To take risks ✳ To achieve anything I put my mind to

Friend 4 ✳ How to be safe ✳ To believe in myself ✳ Loyalty and trust
✳ I am enough ✳ To cut toxic people out of my life

Friend 5 ✳ To talk positively to myself ✳ To hype myself up
✳ To listen more ✳ To let down my walls
✳ To respect people from all walks of life

Ariella Nyssa's Self-love Bible

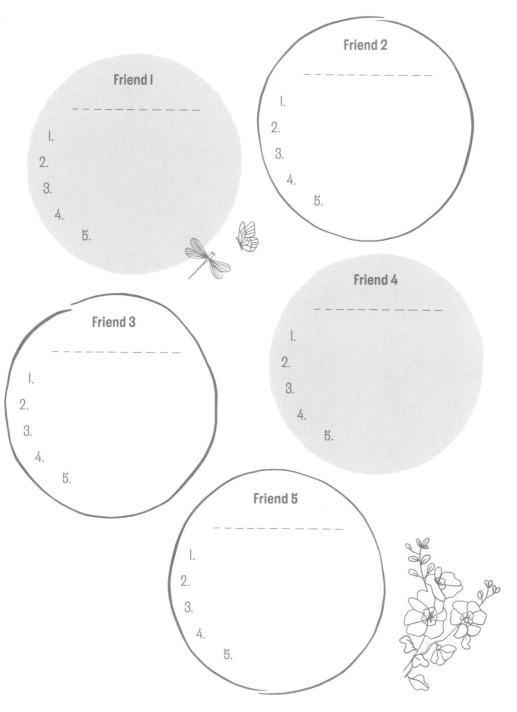

Friend 1

_ _ _ _ _ _ _ _ _ _ _

1.
2.
3.
4.
5.

Friend 2

_ _ _ _ _ _ _ _ _ _ _

1.
2.
3.
4.
5.

Friend 3

_ _ _ _ _ _ _ _ _ _

1.
2.
3.
4.
5.

Friend 4

_ _ _ _ _ _ _ _ _ _ _

1.
2.
3.
4.
5.

Friend 5

_ _ _ _ _ _ _ _ _ _

1.
2.
3.
4.
5.

Your friendship tree

Add the relationships in your life to this friendship tree as roots, branches and leaves. Be as truthful as you can. Trust your intuition and be honest with yourself.

Here's a reminder of what each one means:

＊ **ROOTS** are friendships that are everlasting and sure, that hold you up and keep you grounded.

＊ **BRANCHES** are friendships that are strong but could be broken. They may hold firm for a while but aren't as dependable as they may seem.

＊ **LEAVES** are friendships that come and go with one gust of wind or a change in season.

LETTING GO

Although people can hurt us, we tend to remember the good they've done for us in the past. We have our rose-coloured glasses on. Maybe a friend has changed their priorities, or you have, and your values no longer align. Maybe a friend has been there your whole life, but they are going through their own battles and you feel bad voicing your boundaries. Sometimes, as hard as it is, we need to take off our rose-coloured glasses.

Write a letter to a friend whose friendship is no longer working for you. You don't have to send this to them or show it to anyone; this is just for you. Let go of the guilt and hurt. Let go of the people-pleasing and be real with yourself. Maybe the letter will make you realise that you no longer want to have this friend in your life. Maybe it will make you realise that you need to set firmer boundaries with them. Whatever the case, it's time to let go.

Ariella Nyssa's Self-love Bible

Dear friend,

_____

_____

_____

_____

_____

_____

_____

_____

_____

_____

_____

_____

_____

_____

_____

_____

_____

_____

_____

_____

Love, me

Who is in your inner circle?

Never forget that YOU are the creator of your life. You are the creator of your social geometry. I've heard many times that we become most like the people we surround ourselves with. Your inner circle will define you — and YOU have control over it. Sometimes your circle will decrease, but the *quality* of the people in your circle will increase. Your friends should inspire you, motivate you and support you unconditionally. Surround yourself with people you can grow WITH!

Inside the circle opposite, write the names of everyone who brings positive and amazing attributes to your life. Who is in your inner circle?

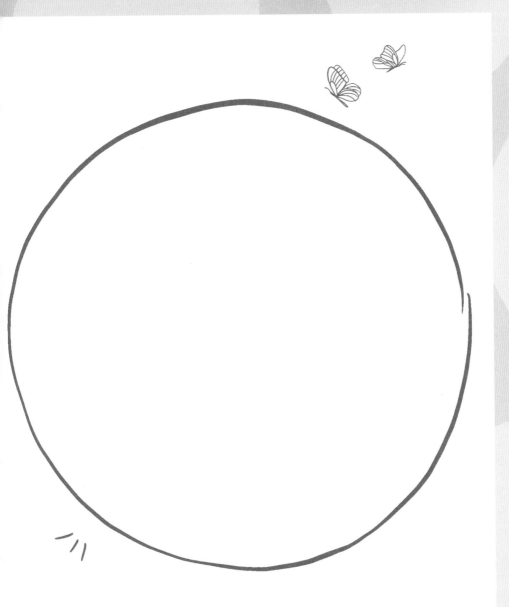

Relationship affirmations

💜 I trust myself to make amazing
and genuine connections.

💜 I trust my intuition in choosing people
who love and support me.

💜 I value my friends and they value me.

💜 I am likeable and loved by so many people.

💜 I deserve to be treated with love,
respect and kindness.

💜 I am setting boundaries to have
relationships that flourish.

💜 I am open to healthy conflict because
it allows me to grow and learn.

THERE IS NOTHING ON THIS EARTH MORE TO BE PREFERRED THAN *friendship.*

THOMAS AQUINAS, *DE REGNO AD REGEM CYPRI*

11

Own your
BELIEFS

When I was really involved in the church, I longed for more all of the time. I was never content or happy within myself and I always thought I needed to be doing more. I thought that I wasn't a 'good enough' Christian if I wasn't 'serving' in the church. In the chaos of those three years that I was fully committed to Christianity and the church, my feelings of guilt imploded. I had at least three nervous breakdowns because I didn't feel good enough for God to love me. I read the Bible every day and prayed morning and night. Sometimes I would fast and I even gave up end-of-school celebrations to go to India on a 'missions' trip, something I now see in a very negative light.

The confronting ideology of heaven and hell hung over my head like a heavy shadow. I truly believed that I would go to hell if I ever tried to seek out new knowledge or even dismiss the idea of God. The guilt I had when I got to high school was even more overwhelming. Purity culture clung to me and if I kissed a boy or talked to someone who wasn't a Christian, I would beg God for forgiveness. I thought I was nothing without my faith or my ideologies. Now, I'm not saying that there is anything wrong with choosing spirituality, or Christianity in general, but I think coming into it at such a young age didn't allow me to form my own perspectives about it all.

When I first left my husband and the church, I was belittled, ridiculed and gossiped about by many people in that community. It deterred me from ever wanting to go back to church and it also deterred me from God. For a while I told people I had my own personal relationship with God, but as time went on and depression took over, I didn't believe in anything anymore.

Over the past five years, I've come to realise that spirituality is different for everyone. Spirituality can be an organised religion or it can be something else entirely. Spirituality isn't about rules and regulations, but about whatever you believe in.

Maybe you have never embarked on your spiritual journey, or maybe you already have a strong sense of it. Either way, exploring and owning what you believe is part of the full story of who you are.

What do you believe?

Spend some time journalling about what you believe and why. Do you believe in a god or gods that control the universe? Do you believe in a higher power? Do you believe that the soul is eternal? Why? You can believe in whatever you want to. This is your freedom. No one is judging. It's time to start having more faith in whatever you believe!

My belief: the 12 laws of the universe

For me, spirituality allows me to live a joyous existence. It allows me to feel gratitude for the small things in life and really experience the journey I'm on. I can be curious and question things around me, big and small. When I first started looking into my spirituality, I started having a greater appreciation for nature and how incredible the world is. Spirituality has allowed me to put my life and struggles into perspective, to think about others more and to acknowledge the energies working around us ALL of the time. Spirituality is different for everyone and that's completely okay! We are all on different journeys. We all have different beliefs and perspectives, and that is beautiful.

To delve into your own spirituality, you must first heal your ego and release any ideals that restrict you from different viewpoints (see Chapter 6). I have found so much contentment and peace in allowing myself to be open to new possibilities.

My belief system includes something called 'the 12 laws of the universe', a set of ideas that are derived from different ancient cultures and can still be used today. These laws have helped me see life from a different perspective. Here's what they are:

LAW OF DIVINE OPENNESS

Everything about you is connected to the universe. Everything is connected. Everything in the universe has its place, as do YOU. This also means that everything we do has a ripple effect. Your actions MATTER and you being here on this Earth makes a difference.

LAW OF VIBRATION

This leads on from the first law. We are all vibrational, everything is vibrational. If we are living in a positive frequency or vibrational state, this means that we will attract similar frequencies or energies.

LAW OF CORRESPONDENCE

If we are stuck in negative routines, self-talk and behaviours, it can have a huge effect on our lives and our decisions. This is why working on accepting our feelings, inner-child work and ego work are so important. We will pick up behaviours from our parents and the people around us without knowing! These routines then get sucked into our subconscious and we are unaware that we are even doing these things. It's so important to become aware so we can break the patterns and move into a more accepting way of being.

LAW OF ATTRACTION

Even though we can't control the world and life around us, there are some practices that have been around for centuries that can help us to attract positive and desired outcomes. The law of attraction is a law that you have most likely heard a lot about. Our thoughts trigger different energies and vibrations in different parts of our brains and thus there is a reaction: the law of attraction is a mirror of our self-worth and thoughts. A key thing to remember is that everything is happening FOR you, not AGAINST you. Be grateful for what you do have, not envious of what you don't.

LAW OF INSPIRED ACTION

This law draws on the law of attraction. To manifest what we truly desire, we must take inspired action! You know the saying 'actions speak louder than words'? This has a direct correlation with the law of inspired action. We need to put motions in place to really achieve what we want in life.

LAW OF PERPETUAL TRANSMUTATION OF ENERGY

This law is reflective of our smallest actions. Every action offers a reaction so even the small things we do have a huge effect! A prime example of this is a seed. In planting a seed, it starts off small. If you water the seed every day, in a few years' time it grows to be a tree or plant. Sometimes we can't see the fruits of our seed, it will take a while to see it in full effect, but it's growing and changing every single day!

LAW OF CAUSE AND EFFECT

Isaac Newton stated that every action has an equal and opposite reaction. This is the case for everything in our lives. It can also be recognised as 'karma' in certain spiritual ideologies. Whatever you put out into the world, you will receive back. Even if you don't believe in karma, you should always strive to be the best version of yourself, which means taking accountability for your actions and always being kind.

LAW OF COMPENSATION

This law is about spreading positivity, love and kindness. If we do this, we will receive compensation for what we sow.

LAW OF RELATIVITY

Right and wrong, good and bad are subjective to each person and their values. It is okay to have different perspectives, and the lesson we can take away from this law is not to carry guilt for things other people have told you are wrong. Me leaving my husband in a Christian community context was deemed wrong by so many people within that community. But it was RIGHT to me: it was the hardest thing I've had to do, but it was right to me.

LAW OF POLARITY

The law of polarity suggests that everything in the universe has a polar opposite, and one cannot exist without the other. Some examples of this are light and dark, good and evil. These notions are dependent on each other; without dark you cannot have light. Without evil you cannot have good. And there is beauty in that.

Have you ever been lost in a really dark room? Maybe you were trying to go to the toilet in the middle of the night and you couldn't find the light switch. Once you flicked on the switch and light filled the room, your fears and anxieties floated away. This to me is the law of polarity and how it helps us to appreciate and show gratitude for the beautiful things in this life.

Ariella Nyssa's Self-love Bible

LAW OF PERPETUAL MOTION

Life is forever transforming and expanding. We are not in control and somehow we are supposed to find peace in that. When I was younger I was a control freak. I liked things to turn out exactly the way I envisioned them, and when they didn't I was left feeling miserable. This is not a sustainable way to live. This drains our spirit. Most likely things are not going to turn out the way we planned. We need to trust the universe and be grateful for what we do have.

THE LAW OF GIVING AND RECEIVING

For centuries the circle or balance of life has functioned under the law of giving and receiving. For example, trees give us oxygen and we give them carbon dioxide. However, the giving and receiving within personal relationships can be one of the most challenging things. When I used to people-please, I was constantly giving to others until I was burned out. I have learned in the last few years that although it's amazing to give to others, we need to also receive!

These 12 laws have helped me to see the world in a completely different light. I have found so much peace in each one of these laws and have integrated them into my life in so many ways. I have been able to forgive myself more, forgive others, be kinder to myself and others, put my life into perspective and show GRATITUDE for even the negative things that occur. I wouldn't be the person I am today without them. That's the thing about journeys, they are like a wild roller-coaster. One second you feel on top of the world and the next you are plummeting down with a knot in your stomach and hanging upside down.

LAWS TO LIVE BY

Choose a few of the 12 laws of the universe from pages 174–177 that resonated with you. How could these laws apply to your own life? Using each law to inspire you, write down some practical steps you can take to tackle negative feelings you have towards yourself or situations in your own life. Be super honest with yourself.

Law:

Law:

Law:

Law: _____
_____
_____
_____
_____

Law: _____
_____
_____
_____
_____
_____

Law: _____
_____
_____
_____
_____
_____

Law: _____
_____
_____
_____
_____

Law: _____
_____
_____
_____
_____

Spirituality affirmations

♥ I am a divine being.

♥ The universe has my back.

♥ I attract positive and amazing things into my life.

♥ I am one with the universe and everything around me.

♥ I am grounded in who I am.

♥ I trust myself.

♥ I am on the right path.

♥ I am a channel for inspiration and enlightenment.

♥ I am always being guided towards my highest good.

♥ I manifest love, peace and kindness into my life.

YOU ARE A MANUSCRIPT
OF A DIVINE LETTER.
YOU ARE A MIRROR
REFLECTING A NOBLE FACE.
THIS UNIVERSE IS NOT
OUTSIDE OF YOU.
Look inside
YOURSELF; EVERYTHING
THAT YOU WANT, YOU ARE
ALREADY THAT.

RUMI

12

stand firm

IN WHO YOU ARE

It's time to get to the pinnacle of you. What do you care most about? And how can you strengthen your love for yourself so that it doesn't crumble when others try to tear you down? I want you to see the beauty in all of yourself, from your physical body to the way you present yourself to the world. This world has torn us all down at one point or another and it's time to unleash our inner power and drown out the negativity that surrounds you.

I have realised over the past few years that I am an empath. I used to see this as a bad thing: why do I care so much about everything? I've been called dramatic, sensitive and too emotional my whole life. These were brought up as criticisms, so I saw my emotions as my enemy. I started to hate that part of myself. But in researching and looking at the true definition of empath, I have realised the beauty in the person I am. The people who were bringing me down about it were projecting their own experiences and insecurities onto me. I decided to embrace what made me different, to harness it as my inner power. Since then, I've been able to reprogram my mind to actively seek out and pursue the things that mean the most to me. For example, I've always placed value on social justice and equality, but used to silence my thoughts because I thought my voice wasn't important enough. When I finally started speaking my truth on social media, I realised that my voice IS important and that change can happen.

Blocking the haters

Sometimes when people aren't coping well, they try to bring others down to make themselves feel better. I get a lot of hate on Instagram and I always used to take it to heart. I would let others' words sink in and they would circle around in my thoughts for months, sometimes even years. People who bully others are more likely to have experienced stressful or traumatic situations in their own lives. When I first found this out, I was able to see those people in a different light. As we self-reflect and work through our own traumas, it can also help us understand why others might lash out.

Whatever the motivation for others tearing you down, it's so important to block their words from entering your subconscious. The only person who knows the honest truth about you is YOU, and even then we all suffer from insecurities that bend our perceptions of our true selves.

What other people say or think about us is a perception of what they see in themselves: *it is not the TRUTH.*

We decide who we want to be in this life. And if we engage in self-reflection and honesty practices with ourselves, we are able to treat ourselves and others with kindness and respect. I have found peace in knowing that not everyone is going to like me, because everyone has lived a completely different life and has their own story.

That said, we also have to be able to distinguish the negative and toxic voices from constructive and useful criticism. Self-awareness is one of the most beneficial things we can do for ourselves and others. It's about looking inwards, reflecting on our actions, listening to people and heaving healthy conflict and discussions. When I started using the hashtag #bodypositivity, for example, I thought it was a phrase that needed to get out more. Little did I know that while I was growing my platform, I was taking up space in a movement that I didn't even know the roots of. I was called out — and rightfully so. But instead of becoming defensive and clapping back at the criticism, I took it on board. I did my own research and realised that I needed to pass the mic. As an able-bodied, thin-passing, white woman in a first-world country, I always knew my privilege, but somewhere along my journey it got pushed to the side. I wanted to fight for the rights of *all* people, but I wasn't showing that in my actions. I realised that I needed to step back and really think about my intentions for my platform and my voice. It is so important to listen.

I am always open to hearing from people I care about or who approach me in a kind and respectful manner. However, I do not let negative and toxic voices in or allow them to penetrate my conscious mind. I set boundaries for myself. I see through to people's true intentions by analysing and self-reflecting. And you need to set boundaries for yourself, too. Listen — really listen — to people. But if you feel that the things they are saying are coming from a place of hate, you need to set boundaries.

You are already whole

Your ego's most powerful weapon is to use layers of guilt complexes accumulated from past experiences and conditioning to create the illusion that you are not whole, that you need to continually pursue outcomes or experiences to make you feel whole, loved and at peace. But the truth is that you are already whole, and at any time you can choose to feel loved and at peace. The trick to it is to become more conscious of areas in your life where you feel guilt, or where you place guilt on others.

When we feel lower-frequency emotions (see page 84), we tend to create scenarios in our heads based on our insecurities. We think that others are thinking this way or viewing us that way. But in reality, everyone's ego is at the forefront of almost everything they do.

If you gave a speech to 100 people, you'd end up with 100 different perceptions of your speech, based on each person's own experiences, relationships and unique views. So if everyone we meet is going to have a completely different opinion of us anyway, why do we get caught up in pleasing everyone?

Other people's opinions of us are none of our business.

Their judgements have nothing to do with us; they are all based on their own perceptions of their reality. This is the ego, and as we stated in previous chapters, it's so important to shift from the ego to your conscious being.

The ancient Chinese philosopher Lao Tse had some advice that some interpret this way: if you care too much about what others think, you will be a prisoner of their opinions. You will never please everyone — and that's okay! I'm sure there are a lot of people in your own life who you haven't gotten along with or agreed with all the time. There are seven billion people on this planet, each one unique, including YOU.

Stand firm in who you are, without the approval of anyone else. You are whole, you are loved, you are worthy.

It's also important to be aware that you are always doing your best at any given time, and that's something to be really proud of. You are living with the knowledge that you have gained up until this point in time, and you are always learning and growing. Don't be so hard on yourself! It's time to see yourself as the beautiful person that you are.

Set boundaries

Spend some time thinking and writing about the questions below.

What are some things that people have put onto you? Maybe they were comments about your cleanliness, your emotions or your kindness? Why do you think you can't let them go?

Who are some people in your life that you need to set boundaries with? Maybe it's a family member, a friend or a neighbour.

And now the harder question: what are your boundaries? Self-reflect and analyse things that may trigger a negative response in you. For example, if your friend is always commenting negatively on your weight, why does that affect you negatively? What boundaries do you need to set with this friend?

WHAT ARE YOUR CORE VALUES?

When I was depressed, I abandoned things that meant a lot to me. Of course, I knew deep down that I cared about those things, but I stopped pursuing them. Out of fear of abandonment, I stopped actively working on myself, researching things I was passionate about and sharing with other people.

Take a few minutes to write answers to the following questions about the things you care about, things you don't want to ever lose sight of. Below are some examples of values that you can use as a starting point to help you decide which ones apply to you.

acceptance COMMITMENT *dependability* equality
FREEDOM honesty *kindness* LOYALTY optimism *passion*
reliability SELF-CARE tolerance *achievement* compassion
ethical family HUMOUR *openness* positivity RESPECT
SELF-EXPRESSION tenacity curiosity EDUCATION *humility*
responsibility *self-confidence* TRUTH creativity service
tradition COMMUNICATION trust

What are your core values?

What are the things that are important to you in your life?

What do you love about yourself?

What are some things you love about yourself? I used to only be able to name a few things that I liked about myself, but I am now able to go on and on and on! This is not vanity, it's self-love. It's so important to be able to see the beautiful things about ourselves and to embrace the people we are! Create a list of all the qualities you appreciate about yourself, whether about your body, your emotions, your values, your skills — anything. Write as many as you can. And don't skip this activity!

Standing firm affirmations

- ♥ I don't care about the negative opinions about me, I know who I am.

- ♥ Other people's opinions of me are not my responsibility.

- ♥ I cut the energetic ties with others who have hurt me or spoken negative words to me.

- ♥ I will dance, speak, live and be free in life, knowing that I create my reality.

WHEN THE SELF AWOKE TO *consciousness,* IT REVEALED THE UNIVERSE OF THOUGHT.

MUHAMMAD IQBAL, *THE SECRETS OF THE SELF*

13

GET *inspired* TO TAKE ACTION

One of my favourite sayings is, 'Actions speak louder than words'. We can self-reflect, journal and talk about things as much as we like — it's a great practice! But it's now time to take action. While working through this book, you have probably had a lot of realisations, and this chapter gives you space to brainstorm and organise some new routines to help you along this self-love journey.

Taking action is imperative when we are trying to create change in our mindsets and self-worth. It may be hard at first, but small steps are the best. Set small goals for yourself each day, and celebrate when you have accomplished them! Many people think you have to make huge, drastic changes to see real growth, but that is not the case at all.

Small steps are what guide us into routines that we'll stick with for life.

To give you an example, here are two things I am working on in my routines:

I. TAKING CARE OF MYSELF

When I got divorced, my depression took over. I stopped looking after myself entirely. And if I'm honest with myself, I still fall into this trap sometimes. I'll 'forget' (on purpose) to look after myself, to drink water or eat nutritious food. I find it really hard sometimes to see my value and thus fall back into old habits. (And it is so true that old habits DIE HARD.) Some new routines I'll be tracking include drinking enough water, eating and maintaining my nutrition, taking my vitamins, taking medicine when I'm sick, sleeping enough, exercising for my mental wellness, meditating and journalling.

2. NOT CARING ABOUT WHAT PEOPLE THINK

I still struggle with this a lot. Not every single day, but my ego still gets swept up in events or experiences from my past that involved a lot of negativity and toxicity. These people are out of my life now, but I still find that I blame myself for the way they treated me. I still hold some of the hurtful words in my subconscious, and I have to keep working on detaching from my ego and forgiving myself and others for everything that happened. I also find it hard to make genuine and strong friendships because sometimes I let my walls bounce back up.

It's time to take the walls down.

It's time to implement strategies and routines to continue letting my past go, letting my worries about the future go and just being in the present moment.

Now it's your turn! On the following pages are guides for daily, weekly and monthly routines, each with an example from me and then a template to copy and fill out for yourself. There are also action templates and some prompts for journal writing. Use these pages to plan out how to implement the ideas from this book into your routine. We can do this!

Monthly, weekly and daily planners

Take a few minutes to plan small goals and activities for your months, weeks and days, thinking about how the way you spend your time ties into the ideas in this book.

Monthly planner

Here's an example of how I might focus my general goals for the month.

Week 1	Week 2
Work on reducing negative self-talk and facing fears	Take care of my body by exercising and drinking more water

Week 3	Week 4
Work on forgiveness (of myself and others)	Find things to be thankful for

My monthly planner

Your turn!

Week 1

Week 2

Week 3

Week 4

Weekly planner

Here's an example of how I might focus my activities for week one of my monthly plan.

Monday	Become aware of my inner critic. Try to notice every time I put myself down.
Tuesday	Whenever I notice negative self-talk, try to reframe the thought.
Wednesday	Think about something I'd love to do but am afraid to. What is holding me back?
Thursday	Write a letter to myself, encouraging me to face my fear.
Friday	Write down one tiny step I could take to face my fear.
Saturday	Take that one tiny step. If it feels good, write down the next tiny step.
Sunday	Spend some time journalling and celebrating what I have achieved this week.

My weekly planner

Your turn!

Monday	
Tuesday	
Wednesday	
Thursday	
Friday	
Saturday	
Sunday	

Daily planner

Here's an example of how I might plan one of the days in my weekly planner, working on the specific goals for that day, week and month, as well as on my goals in general. On the next pages, there's a blank planner for you to copy and fill with your own goals and activities.

6 am	Wake up and repeat my affirmations
7 am	Get outside, drink a coffee and have my breakfast (self-care, being present in nature)
8 am	Take the dogs for a walk
9 am	Do the daily activity from my weekly planner
10 am	Get dressed and ready for the day, then work (productivity)
1 pm	Lunch break: eat a nutritious yummy meal, drink water (self-care)
2 pm	Listen to a podcast or music, or read a book (creativity, enlightenment)

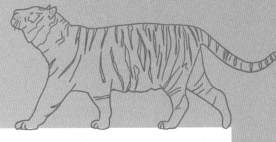

3 pm	Spend time with loved ones (positive relationships)
4 pm	Work out (self-care)
5 pm	Cook and eat a nutritious dinner (self-care)
6 pm	Wind down for the day by journalling, painting, stretching or watching a favourite show (being present, valuing my uniqueness)
8 pm	Shower, drink tea or eat a yummy dessert (self-care)
9 pm	Read a book, talk to friends, spend time with pets and loved ones (positive relationships)
10 pm	Hop into bed for a good night's sleep (self-care)

Get inspired to take action

My daily planner

Your turn!

6 am	
7 am	
8 am	
9 am	
10 am	
11 am	
12 am	
1 pm	

Ariella Nyssa's Self-love Bible

2 pm	
3 pm	
4 pm	
5 pm	
6 pm	
7 pm	
8 pm	
9 pm	
10 pm	

ACTION TEMPLATES

Now that you've read this book, what are the problems or issues you've identified in your life? What actions do you want to take to deal with them? Thinking through each one, write down what it is ('topic'), your thoughts about it and the action you'd like to take. Here's an example from me:

Topic	→	Thoughts	→	Action
Difficult childhood memories		These self-hating thoughts are a result of the bullying I got at school.		Whenever I self-criticise, stop and think of something positive about myself.

Topic	→	Thoughts	→	Action

Topic	→	Thoughts	→	Action

Topic	→	Thoughts	→	Action

Topic	→	Thoughts	→	Action

Topic	→	Thoughts	→	Action

Topic	→	Thoughts	→	Action

Journal prompts

Use the following prompts to inspire yourself whenever you feel like journalling.

✳ **How do you feel today?**

✳ What's on your mind?

✳ **Who are you thinking about today?**

✳ What are your worries?

✳ **What makes you feel powerful?**

✳ What makes you feel calm?

✳ **How can you encourage yourself when you are doing something new?**

✳ How do you recharge?

Inspired action affirmations

♥ I am proud of the small steps I have taken
to grow and become my true self.

♥ I do not feel guilty for falling; I always get back up.

♥ I am always making decisions to better myself.

♥ I take care of my body, soul and mind.

♥ I always do what's best for me.

All my love

Writing this book has been a wild roller-coaster. It has brought up past trauma, helped me heal and made me realise how much I have grown. As hard as some of those times were, I see clearly now that all of it has happened to make me the person that I am today.

Life is an incredible thing. Sometimes it's something we all take for granted, but it's so important to focus on the positives and be grateful for everything we have achieved so far. I'm always open to learning and growing, and I'm so grateful for the journey that I have been on.

I hope that through this journey, you can see how special and worthy YOU are, too. I'm proud of myself and I'm so proud of you!

YOU ARE A CHILD OF THE *universe* NO LESS THAN THE TREES AND THE STARS; YOU HAVE A RIGHT TO BE HERE.

MAX EHRMANN,
'DESIDERATA'

Reflection

Take some time to reflect on and journal about the following questions.

What have you learned about yourself while working through this book? _____

_____

_____

_____

_____

_____

_____

_____

What have you realised about self-love? _____

_____

_____

_____

_____

_____

_____

What steps are you going to take to transform your mind, soul and body? _____

_____

_____

_____

_____

_____

_____

What are your aspirations for the future? _____

_____

_____

_____

_____

_____

What are you proud of? _____

_____

_____

_____

_____

_____

_____

Support
YOUR
HEALING

RITUALS TO SUPPORT GROWTH

I want to leave you with some activities to open your perspective even further. These are amazing rituals that I use daily and that have brought me to such a confident and peaceful state of mind.

Mirror work

A mirror reflects back to you the feelings that you have about yourself. Mirror work is an amazing practice that you can use to self-reflect and learn to love every inch of your being. It was developed by inspirational teacher Louise Hay and was designed to help us get in touch with our inner selves. It's such a simple practice that can guide us more in our self-love, and you only have to set aside a few minutes every day. This routine will ground you and allow you to develop your relationship with yourself and others on a whole new level.

Sit or stand in front of your mirror for just five minutes. Set a timer on your phone and stare at yourself, maintaining eye contact.

Pay attention to how you feel. Do you feel uncomfortable? Awkward? It may bring up feelings of resentment and self-hatred, or you might even criticise different parts of your being. It may bring up old memories or traumas. But I just want you to sit with the feelings, as uncomfortable as they may be. Louise Hay explained why this is so normal for a lot of us. She said that in front of a mirror, there is no hiding. The mirror makes you aware of what you are resisting and where you are open and flowing. It shows you what thoughts you need to change in your journey of self-love. It sheds light on the inner critic and saboteur that lives in each of our subconscious minds. We may not even know that this critic exists, or it may whisper in our ear from time to time.

Mirror work is a powerful, transformative tool that allows us to heal our inner child and wounds, and move into a deeper form of self-love. Use it as a daily routine for healing, transformation and a deeper understanding of who you are!

Spiritual bath and cleansing

Water serves as a powerful healing tool in many cultures. Our bodies are 50 to 60 per cent water, so it makes sense that it is a useful thing for us. Water can be used to cleanse us from unhealthy habits, heal us from traumas and wash away our anxiety. This routine only takes 10 to 20 minutes of your day and is a great way to reconnect with your soul and self-love.

Create a loving and supportive space in your bathroom. I use crystals, candles, bath bombs and essential oils to create a peaceful atmosphere. Start to run the water into the bath and close your eyes. Imagine that the water holds transformative emotions: love, peace, compassion, support, wholeness, healing. As the water runs, set an intention for your session. This can be anything that you want to release or let go of in your own life, perhaps fear, people-pleasing, past trauma or anything that is unsettling you. By setting an intention and visualising the energy from the running water, you are creating space for self-love and enlightenment. Before you get into the bath, pop in the essential oils and gently stir the water around with your hand or foot. As you do this, choose an affirmation to support your intention. I have put a few affirmations at the end of each chapter, so if any resonated with you choose one of those, or even make up your own. Immerse yourself in the bath and repeat your chosen affirmations as the water covers your body. Close your eyes, breathe and really believe in the power of your words. Take time to wash and cleanse your body and enjoy!

Get grounded in nature

Grounding is an amazing practice to connect you back to nature and to your true self. It balances your spiritual energy with your physical energy and is also a great way to be in the present moment.

You can ground yourself in nature at any time on any day that you want and there are so many different ways to do it. I love to go and find a quiet place and walk around barefoot. I feel the grass, sand or dirt between my toes and close my eyes. Go find a beautiful tree or big patch of grass and sit down. Imagine roots and vines growing from your hands and feet as you push them into the ground. Another amazing thing to do is to walk around in a forest, bush or garden and gently feel the plants, trees and flowers. Take some time to be present with nature and be thankful for each and every living thing. Hug a tree. Smell a flower. Be present outside and allow the earth to strengthen your power and energy.

Dance

I have been to a few ecstatic dance events and they are the biggest release. When we dance in public or when there are people around, we usually feel insecure or awkward. Think about a nightclub. Everyone is on their best behaviour, bopping around, criticising themselves and others. Dance is such an incredible way to release your anxiety and fear of what others think of you. The events that I have gone to have brought me to the point of tears — happy tears, knowing that I am finally being myself, my walls have come down and I am just being ME. Of course, you don't have to go to an event to do this. I do this in my very own bedroom or outside on a walk. The premise of the ritual is to let go of fear and bring out your inner child.

Find a space ANYWHERE. This can be at home, in a garden, on a walk or even with a group of friends! Sit down and meditate for ten minutes before you begin. Close your eyes and think of an intention for the session. It could be a few of the following or you can even make up your own:

✳ I release fear and anxiety from my life.

✳ I don't want to fear other people's judgements anymore.

✳ I want to let more fun into my life.

✳ I want to learn to love myself more.

✳ I want to be grounded in who I am.

Put on any kind of music you like, but make sure you include slow, medium- and fast-paced music so you can move your body in different rhythms. And ... DANCE. There's no right or wrong way to do this. The point of this ritual is to completely LET GO. Let go of your ego, your identity and just be. You might even let out a scream or sound to release tension while you dance. And if you're dancing with someone else, try staring into each other's eyes for a few seconds.

SERVICES TO SUPPORT HEALING

When I was in a dark place, I was doing things on my own. I tried implementing all I was reading and learning, but sometimes it wasn't enough. Sometimes I needed help. And it's completely okay to ask for help and guidance. Here are a few different ways you can acknowledge and ask for professional help. You don't need to do this alone.

Counsellors, psychologists and psychiatrists

I know therapy isn't for everyone, but it really helped me and a lot of other people in my life. You may not know where to start, you may think that talking about things will bring trauma back up. But to live in a constant state of fear, anxiety and low self-worth can hold you back from stepping into your light and realising the gift you are to this Earth. It breaks my heart to think that any of you wonderful angels are living in a constant state of self-loathing or heartbreak: you deserve better. If you feel like this book is bringing up trauma for you, I encourage you to see a counsellor, a psychologist or a psychiatrist. Looking after your mental health isn't weak. Your feelings are justified and important; you deserve to feel heard.

FIND YOUR NEAREST PSYCHOLOGIST:

Australian Association of Psychologists Inc: aapi.org.au or 0488 770 044
New Zealand Psychological Society: psychology.org.nz/public/find-psychologist
The British Psychological Society: bps.org.uk/public/find-psychologist
American Psychological Association: locator.apa.org or 800 374 2721

Mental health and crisis support

If you are thinking about suicide, or feeling that you just can't cope with life any more, call one of these services. Even if it's not an emergency, sometimes it's nice to just talk to someone, for someone to listen.

AUSTRALIA

Lifeline: lifeline.org.au or 13 11 14
Beyond Blue: beyondblue.org.au
*   or 1300 22 46 36*
Kids Helpline: kidshelpline.com.au
*   or 1800 55 1800*

NEW ZEALAND

Lifeline Aotearoa: lifeline.org.nz
*   or 0800 543 354*

UNITED KINGDOM

Samaritans: samaritans.org
*   or 116 123*
SupportLine: supportline.org.uk
*   or 01708 765 200*

UNITED STATES

National Suicide Prevention Lifeline:
*   suicidepreventionlifeline.org*
*   or 1800 273 8255*
Crisis Text Line: crisistextline.org
*   or text HOME to 741 741*

Doctors

Our health is holistic. Health is definitely a factor in so many aspects of our self-love journeys. When I was going through a lot, I starved myself and then binged. I ate foods I was intolerant of. I was low in vitamins and nutrients. I didn't drink water and I didn't think I mattered enough to take care of my being. It's important to check in with a doctor to make sure you are looking after yourself, on all levels: mentally, spiritually, physically, emotionally.

FIND YOUR NEAREST DOCTOR:

AUSTRALIA healthdirect.gov.au/australian-health-services
NEW ZEALAND healthpoint.co.nz
UNITED KINGDOM nhs.uk/service-search/find-a-gp
UNITED STATES usa.gov/doctors

Spiritual healers

Spiritual healers have changed my life. The first time I went to one, I didn't really understand the concept or what was going to happen in our session, but I stepped into the unknown and I'm so glad I did. As soon as I walked in the door, my healer intuitively sensed a lot of the blockages within my body. We spoke about chakras (a concept that arose in India between 1500 and 500 BC) and we delved into the way they relate to different parts of our bodies and how they can be blocked. These focal points can be traced back to the early traditions of Hinduism. The chakras are:

✳ **The heart chakra in your chest. It is reflective of love, peace, compassion, acceptance and kindness.**

✳ The solar plexus chakra in your belly. It is reflective of confidence and self-esteem.

✳ **The throat chakra in your throat/neck. It is reflective of communication, honesty, expression and purification.**

✳ The sacral chakra in your sacrum. It is reflective of creativity, sexuality, sensuality, emotions and pleasure.

✳ **The root chakra in your perineum. It is reflective of survival, stability, grounding, comfort and safety.**

✳ The crown chakra at the top of your head. It is reflective of knowledge, intelligence, self-realisation, spirituality and fulfilment.

✳ **The third eye chakra in between your eyes. It is reflective of imagination, clairvoyance, intuition and visualisation.**

When our chakras are blocked, it can cause physical, mental and emotional disruptions. My spiritual healer told me that my root chakra and my heart chakra were blocked, which meant that I was holding on to experiences or negativity that was affecting all levels of my life. My blocked heart chakra meant that I was closed off to people around me. It affected my relationships and my own security in opening up to new people. My blocked root chakra meant that fear and different forms of trauma made me disconnected from my physical body. I was experiencing anxiety, panic attacks, fear, worry, overthinking and nightmares. She then took me through visualisation of cutting the ties between past relationships and traumas that were living in my subconscious.

I cried the whole time; the whole hour and a half I sobbed — but it was a HAPPY cry. It was the first time I had allowed myself to be truly emotional about all of the relationships that had broken down in my life, and to fully forgive myself and others. It was the release I needed. I truly felt like myself for the first time in so long. I realised my potential and what thoughts and feelings had been negatively impacting me. I finally let go of any guilt and felt like ME again. It was euphoric.

I was so delightfully shocked with the outcome of my first spiritual session that I have since looked into other spiritual healing practices. For example, reiki, also known as energy healing, is a Japanese form of alternative medicine that is also incredible. We are all energy, and this form of healing focuses on transmitting a universal energy through the palms of the healer to the person being healed.

It's so important to do your own research about spiritual healing. As I've said throughout this book, this is my journey. You have your own unique and inspiring journey, and the things that worked for me may not be things you are interested in. But I encourage you to open your perspectives and try new things. Try to find different ways of healing. Talk to someone or change the routines that have been embedded into your life and limit you from seeing your worth and healing.

Healing affirmations

♥ I take up space and I step into my purpose.

♥ I deserve to feel heard and my feelings are justified.

♥ I acknowledge that my mental health is important
and I'm going to work on healing.

♥ I embrace my sexuality, my spiritual beliefs and who I am.

♥ I am important enough to allow others to help me.

♥ Asking for help is okay and everyone needs guidance sometimes.

♥ I embrace my body, my mind and my soul, and I embrace my journey.

♥ Everything that has happened in my life has led me to
this moment and made me who I am today.

♥ I trust in the universe and I trust myself.

♥ I am worthy and divine.

♥ I deserve to feel peace and to love myself from the inside out.

WHEN WE CHANGE OUR *nature,* THE WORLD AROUND SHOULD ALSO INEVITABLY CHANGE.

**MAHATMA GANDHI,
*A GUIDE TO HEALTH***

ACKNOWLEDGEMENTS

First of all, I want to say thank you to myself: past, present and future. Thank you for believing in me when no one else did. Thank you for sticking around and not giving up. I appreciate you and I love you.

Christopher, you are the light in my life. Thank you for the outpouring of love you have given me from the second we met. You saw so much more in me than I could ever see in myself. You pulled me up out of the darkest hole and showed me that loving life again was possible. You blow me away with your positive energy and that you wholeheartedly accept me for who I am. Thank you for being the inspiration and motivator behind this book; for sitting with me for hours on end, coming up with ideas and motivating me to finish it. Thank you for reading it and loving every inch of it. Thank you for being you: I don't know where I would be without you.

My family have stood by me through everything: my mum, dad and brother Zac supported me through my darkest times and encouraged me to be my best and truest self. Thank you. I LOVE you with all of my heart and am so grateful to have you all as my family.

My cousin Tam, thank you for loving me for who I am and thank you for being my sister. Thank you for being honest with me in the tougher times and thank you for believing in me. I love you.

To my Murdoch Books team, thank you for pushing me to be the best version of myself possible. For connecting all of my ideas, designs and creations. For creating exactly what I wanted my *Self-love Bible* to look like. Thank you for the hours you have put into this. And thank you for making all of my dreams come true.

I just want to acknowledge all of the people who tore me down until I felt like I was nothing. Thank you. It's taken me a long time to get to this place, where I can thank you for what you tried to do to me. If you hadn't done it, I would never have done this; I would have never been the person that I was meant to be. So thank you. Thank you for helping me to realise my full potential and to accept and love who I truly am.

Ariella xx

INDEX OF ACTIVITIES

RECOMMENDED READING, LISTENING & VIEWING

Brian Tracy briantracy.com

Eckhart Tolle eckharttolle.com; *The Power of Now* (Hachette Australia, 2018)

Esther Hicks abraham-hicks.com

Joe Dispenza drjoedispenza.com; *Breaking the Habit of Being Yourself* (Hay House Inc., 2013)

Louise Hay louisehay.com

Novalee Wilder novaleewilder.com

SOURCES

page 39 Gautama Buddha, *Dhammapada*, 'The Thousands' verses 103–104

page 63 Hermann Hesse, *Siddhartha*, Part II, 'The Ferryman'

page 75 Joseph Conrad, *Typhoon*, Chapter V

page 95 John Milton, *Paradise Lost*, Book I, lines 233–234

page 105 George Washington, in a letter to Mary Ball Washington, Mount Vernon, 15 February 1787

page 117 Henry David Thoreau, journal entry for 24 April 1859

page 127 Mohandas K. Gandhi, *Young India*, 2 April 1931

page 139 Ralph Waldo Emerson, *Society and Solitude: Twelve Chapters*, 'Success'

page 151 Lao Tse, *Tao Te Ching*, Part I, 80:4

page 169 Thomas Aquinas, *De regno ad regem Cypri*, Book I, Chapter 2:77

page 181 Rumi, Quatrains

page 195 Muhammad Iqbal, *The Secrets of the Self*, translated by Reynold A. Nicholson, Book I, lines 189–190

page 212 Max Ehrmann, 'Desiderata'

page 227 Mahatma Gandhi, *A Guide to Health*, 'Accident—Snake Bite'

Published in 2022 by Murdoch Books,
an imprint of Allen & Unwin

Murdoch Books Australia
83 Alexander Street
Crows Nest NSW 2065
Phone: +61 (0)2 8425 0100
murdochbooks.com.au
info@murdochbooks.com.au

Murdoch Books UK
Ormond House
26–27 Boswell Street
London WC1N 3JZ
Phone: +44 (0) 20 8785 5995
murdochbooks.co.uk
info@murdochbooks.co.uk

For corporate orders and custom publishing,
contact our business development team at
salesenquiries@murdochbooks.com.au

Publisher: Lou Johnson
Editorial Manager: Julie Mazur Tribe
Design Manager: Megan Pigott
Designer: Madeleine Kane
Editor: Melody Lord
Photographer: Christopher Mott
Illustrator: Julia Cornelius
Production Director: Lou Playfair

We acknowledge that we meet and work on the
traditional lands of the Cammeraygal people
of the Eora Nation and pay our respects to their
elders past, present and future.

ISBN 978 1 92235 195 1

 A catalogue record for this
book is available from the
National Library of Australia

A catalogue record for this book is available
from the British Library

Colour reproduction by Splitting Image
Colour Studio Pty Ltd, Clayton, Victoria
Printed by C&C Offset Printing Co. Ltd., China

DISCLAIMER: The content presented in this
book is meant for inspiration and informational
purposes only. The author and publisher claim
no responsibility to any person or entity for any
liability, loss, or damage caused or alleged to be
caused directly or indirectly as a result of the
use, application, or interpretation of the material
in this book.

10 9 8 7 6 5 4 3 2 1

MIX
Paper from
responsible sources
FSC® C008047